Oxford School *Shakespeare*

MEASURE *for* MEASURE

edited by
Roma Gill, OBE
M.A. *Cantab.*, B. Litt. *Oxon*

OXFORD
UNIVERSITY PRESS

OXFORD
UNIVERSITY PRESS
Great Clarendon Street, Oxford OX2 6DP

Oxford University Press is a department of the University of Oxford. It furthers the University's objective of excellence in research, scholarship, and education by publishing worldwide in

Oxford New York

Athens Auckland Bangkok Bogotá Buenos Aires Calcutta Cape Town Chennai Dar es Salaam Delhi Florence Hong Kong Istanbul Karachi Kuala Lumpur Madrid Melbourne Mexico City Mumbai Nairobi Paris São Paulo Shanghai Singapore Taipei Tokyo Toronto Warsaw

with associated companies in Berlin Ibadan

OXFORD is a registered trade mark of Oxford University Press in the UK and in certain other countries

ISBN 0 19 832009 4 (Schools edition) 1 3 5 7 9 10 8 6 4 2
ISBN 0 19 832010 8 (Trade edition) 1 3 5 7 9 10 8 6 4 2

Illustrations by Alexy Pendle

All photographs by Donald Cooper (Photostage). Cover shows Stella Gonet as Isabella and Michael Feast as the Duke in the Royal Shakespeare Company's 1994 Stratford production of *Measure for Measure*

For Rebecca

Oxford School Shakespeare
edited by Roma Gill

A Midsummer Night's Dream	Othello
Romeo and Juliet	Hamlet
As You Like It	King Lear
Macbeth	Henry V
Julius Caesar	The Winter's Tale
The Merchant of Venice	The Tempest
Henry IV Part I	Antony and Cleopatra
Twelfth Night	Richard II
The Taming of the Shrew	Coriolanus
Measure for Measure	Much Ado About Nothing

Typeset by Herb Bowes Graphics, Oxford
Printed by Alden Press Limited

Contents

Introduction

About the Play

Sex—or your brother dies! It's a terrible choice—and this rapist is no ordinary thug but the most respectable, most powerful man in the land. His victim is not only young and inexperienced: she's so devoutly religious that she is about to become a nun.

There's nothing new about governmental hypocrisy and sexual corruption in high places. Is there anyone nowadays who believes that those in authority are always above reproach in their private lives, or that men (and women) in positions of power will not sometimes exploit those powers for their own ends? *Measure for Measure* is a sensitive exploration of what happens when a government minister with an otherwise unblemished reputation suddenly finds himself exposed to temptation, unable to control his passions, and with all the means of enforcing them.

Shakespeare bases his play on an old story, giving it a setting in a city of sleaze and sin which he calls 'Vienna' but which, in its social details, could well be his own contemporary London—or any other capital city, now or at any time.

In this Vienna there are rumours of war, but these are never realized, and the men who might have gone off to fight have nothing better to do than lounge about the streets, swapping good-natured insults. Sexually transmitted disease has become something of a joke, and the local brothel's trade is managing to survive. The prison is fairly full, but the offenders are mainly petty crooks and fraudsters—although there are a few long-term criminals whose cases are being dragged out by the tedious legal system. The constabulary seems to be dependent on a single officer, whose energy is only equalled by his stupidity; the governor of the prison and the senior Justice are two kindly, tolerant old men; and the head of state, the duke, has for a long time been more interested in his reading than in the responsibilities of his position.

Stagnation! But now the duke has found the right man to carry out a long overdue clean-up job—Lord Angelo. He may not have much practical experience of government, but he is (on paper) extremely well qualified, and his personal reputation is apparently spotless. Angelo sets himself up as a model of righteous behaviour, strict in his judgements and so confident in himself that he is prepared to be judged by his own standards.

> When I that censure him do so offend
> Let mine own judgement pattern out my death.
>
> (2, 1, 29–30)

This is the teaching of the Bible (although Angelo does not acknowledge it) from which Shakespeare's play takes its title—

> Judge not, that ye be not judged. For with what judgement ye judge, ye shall be judged: and with what measure ye mete, it shall be measured to you again. (Matthew 7:1–2)

Angelo should be careful! His confidence could prove dangerous, and even tragic . . .

But this play, which ends with three (perhaps four) weddings and no funerals, is not a tragedy. Shakespeare manages to achieve the conventionally 'happy' outcome of a comedy for all the dilemmas his plot has created—but he cannot provide any harmonious solutions for the problems it has raised and which increasingly worry modern directors. *Measure for Measure*, along with *Troilus and Cressida* and *All's Well That Ends Well*, has been called[1] a 'Problem Play' because it resists attempts to label it as 'tragedy' or 'comedy', and because it leaves its audiences and readers with more questions than when it started. What controls are necessary for social living—and whose responsibility is it to operate these? Where and when is judgement possible—and who should be the judge? Don't we all make judgements on others, all the time—and is this always wrong? Does all power corrupt? Must all liberty become licence? How can we limit the spread of sexually transmitted disease? What hope for the young and innocent . . . ?

Shakespeare's own opinions and sympathies are—typically—hard to determine, although his plays show that he always abhorred hypocrisy, and he must surely have deplored widespread sexual promiscuity and its attendant ills. None of the characters in *Measure for Measure* is perfect—like Barnardine, they are all 'desperately mortal'

[1]By F. S. Boas in *Shakespeare and his Predecessors* (1896).

(4, 2, 136)—but Shakespeare condemns none and finds some good in all—even in the drunken, unrepentant murderer, who can still assert his human right not to be executed for the duke's convenience. Perhaps there is a particular kindness in the dramatist's treatment of the naive young Claudio and his girlfriend Juliet, for Shakespeare himself, it seems, had once been guilty like them of careless loving: he was only eighteen when he married Anne Hathaway in 1582 (some twenty years before he wrote this play), and Anne was already three months pregnant with their first child.

Leading Characters in the Play

The Duke An ambiguous figure of some mystery, who has neglected the government of Vienna and now leaves Angelo to clean up whilst he is away—but attempts to stage-manage the action from behind his disguise as a friar.

Angelo The deputy chosen by the duke to govern in his absence is very highly qualified, with a reputation for puritanical conduct and ideas. But his integrity is going to be tested.

Escalus A wise counsellor who is placed second-in-command to Angelo and who attempts to moderate his judgements.

Claudio A rather naive young man who has been condemned to death for getting his girlfriend, Juliet, pregnant.

Isabella Claudio's sister, passionate in defence of her chastity, and eager to join a strict order of nuns.

Lucio An idle gentleman of casual morality whose friendship saves Claudio from execution.

Pompey Tapster and pimp from Mistress Overdone's brothel—and the voice of common sense on matters of sex.

Synopsis

Act 1

Scene 1 The Duke of Vienna delegates his authority to Angelo.

Scene 2 Lucio and his friends meet Mistress Overdone and learn that Claudio has been condemned to death by Angelo. Claudio needs help from his sister, and sends Lucio with a message.

Scene 3 The duke confides in Friar Thomas, then disguises himself as a friar.

Scene 4 Lucio tells Isabella about Claudio's predicament and enlists her help.

Act 2

Scene 1 Angelo and Escalus hold a trial, but Elbow's evidence is muddled, and Angelo becomes impatient. Froth is given a warning by Escalus, and Pompey gets a caution.

Scene 2 Isabella pleads with Angelo for her brother's life, but her words only excite Angelo's lust.

Scene 3 The duke, in his friar's disguise, visits the prison and meets Juliet.

Scene 4 Isabella comes back to plead with Angelo, who makes a proposition—and a threat.

Act 3

Scene 1 Counselling Claudio, the 'friar' overhears Isabella when she tells her brother of Angelo's proposition, and he makes plans to thwart the duke's deputy.

Scene 2 The 'friar' encounters Pompey and hears Lucio slandering the duke; he meets Mistress Overdone, discusses the world with Escalus, and outlines his next scheme to the audience.

Act 4

Scene 1 The 'friar' and Isabella enlist Mariana's aid in tricking Angelo.

Scene 2 Pompey finds new employment in prison. The 'friar' and the provost wait for Claudio's reprieve, but they are disappointed. New plans are made to satisfy Angelo's demand for Claudio's head.

Scene 3 Barnardine refuses to be hanged as a substitute for Claudio, but a replacement is found. Lucio continues to slander the duke.

Scene 4 Angelo and Escalus are bewildered by the duke's letters.

Scene 5 The duke continues to make arrangements.

Scene 6 Isabella and Mariana discuss their instructions.

Act 5

Scene 1 The duke returns to Vienna. Isabella accuses Angelo—and is sent to prison. The duke disappears. Escalus will not believe Mariana until she reveals her identity. The duke reappears in his friar's disguise, and Lucio repeats his slanders—then discovers his mistake. Angelo confesses all, but Mariana and Isabella plead for his life. Lucio is condemned to matrimony!

Measure for Measure: commentary

Act 1

Scene 1 What's going on? For reasons of his own, the duke must get away from Vienna as quickly as possible. He entrusts all his powers to Angelo, a junior minister, warning him about the conduct that will be expected of him, and makes a hurried and unceremonious getaway—leaving behind him two very puzzled government officials, and an audience perplexed in the extreme.

The duke's language, heavy with metaphors and biblical overtones, seems to be saying very much more than we can immediately understand, whilst the strained syntax of his verse gives the impression that the duke himself may be under some stress or embarrassment. His chosen deputy is apparently reluctant to take on such responsibility, and speaks little; but Angelo's colleague, Escalus, shows himself to be the true figure of an elder statesman, offering deference without resentment to the younger man promoted above him.

In these inner chambers of government the atmosphere is stuffy with repressive formality, but soon we are outside, in the real world of Vienna—

Scene 2 —where we find that the duke has left behind him a city of sleaze. Lucio and his friends are casually joshing each other as they discuss current affairs, but the horrors of venereal disease are never far from their thoughts, even in jest, and especially when they are joined by the local brothel-keeper, Mistress Overdone, with her news about the latest piece of legislation.

Angelo has not been slow in making his presence felt. An old law curtailing sexual liberty has been revived, and already under this law a young man, Claudio, has been condemned to death for getting his girlfriend pregnant. Laughter ceases, and the gossips hurry to check out this unwelcome piece of information, leaving Mistress Overdone—and the audience—to hear the latest details of this depressing situation from Pompey, her tapster and part-time pimp.

The irrepressible Pompey refuses to be downhearted. Although Angelo intends to pull down all 'houses of resort' in the city, Mistress Overdone needn't change her trade—just her address! The approach of the provost sends them scurrying away; and the audience sees the truth of the rumours they have heard.

The provost is followed by two prisoners—Claudio, deeply embarrassed by this public humiliation, and his girlfriend Juliet, speechless in her misery, and heavily pregnant. With Claudio's first words a new tone enters the play. Emotional truth and urgency speak through the rhythms and imagery as he explains his predicament to Lucio—although the calm wisdom of his philosophical, unquestioning acceptance of Angelo's judgement is surprising:

> Our natures do pursue
> Like rats that ravin down their proper bane
> A thirsty evil, and when we drink, we die.

He has done what is only natural—'proper' to human nature; but it may well prove as fatal for him as the thirst-provoking poison used for killing rats.

Marriages in Shakespeare's day were hedged around with legal complications, and the play's original audiences would have found it easy to understand the situation that Claudio now describes: legally contracted to each other, he and Juliet had been waiting only for financial arrangements to be completed before their marriage was declared official. Angelo, however, to get a reputation for himself, is going to make an example of Claudio, whose only hope now lies in his sister's powers of persuasion ('she hath prosperous art When she will play with reason and discourse'). Lucio is a willing messenger, loath to have his friend's life 'foolishly lost at a game of tick-tack'.

Scene 3 Why has the duke left Vienna and its citizens in such disarray? Why was the clean-up campaign delegated to a subordinate—and does the duke really know what kind of man he has chosen?

The duke begins to explain himself to Friar Thomas—or, rather, to make excuses for himself: he has 'ever lov'd the life remov'd' and has now handed over the reins of government to Lord Angelo, known to be a man 'of stricture and firm abstinence'. Although he begins by speaking with the direct pronoun 'I', the duke slips easily into the 'royal plural' (which is also the evasive plural that disowns responsibility) when he speaks of the laws which 'for this fourteen years we have let slip' and which have become a mockery for malefactors. Friar Thomas is not deceived: 'It rested in your grace To unloose this tied-up justice when you pleas'd', and it should be the duke's responsibility to restore the situation to its proper order.

But the duke is determined that Angelo shall have the unenviable task of cleaning up the city—whilst he himself, disguised as a friar, will keep watch over his apparently 'precise' deputy:

Hence shall we see,
If power change purpose, what our seemers be.

This takes the audience, as well as Friar Thomas, into the duke's confidence: some sort of experiment is being tried, but everything will be under control.

Scene 4 Nuns of the Order of St Clare (popularly known as the 'Poor Clares') are subject to the strictest of disciplines—but even this is not enough for the enthusiastic young novice, Claudio's sister. Isabella shows no surprise when she hears Lucio's news, and is quick with a solution for Claudio's predicament—'Someone with child by him? My cousin Juliet? . . . O, let him marry her'. What Claudio has done is accepted, by Isabella and Lucio alike, as the most natural of deeds, associated with life and rich fertility, 'blossoming time' and 'teeming foison'. Angelo's chilling justice, by contrast, comes from one 'whose blood Is very snow-broth' and who is immune to those same 'wanton stings and motions of the sense' which have quickened into such new life for Claudio.

Prompted by Lucio, Isabella hurries towards Angelo.

Act 2

Scene 1 'Wouldn't you have done the same?' In the courtroom Escalus is trying to persuade Angelo to look more sympathetically on Claudio's 'crime', but the duke's deputy is unmovable—

'Tis one thing to be tempted, Escalus,
Another thing to fall.

—and he will continue to uphold his sentence on Claudio, offering Escalus a model of jurisdiction:

When I that censure him do so offend
Let mine own judgement pattern out my death.

To forestall any further discussion of this topic, he accelerates the process of the law by demanding its immediate execution.

There is other business now before the two magistrates. Elbow the constable, bumbling and self-important in his high office, presents for trial 'two notorious benefactors', Pompey and Froth. All the earlier tension evaporates into laughter with Elbow's verbal mistakings ('malapropisms'): we remember that the duke is really in control—and now it seems there is a comic spirit in the air!

Pompey, accused of pimping for Mistress Overdone, is not in the least overawed in this legal presence and defends himself with gusto, offering a confusion of precisely recollected irrelevant details, and hints of diseases unmentionable in polite society. The justices themselves are the first to be tried. Angelo soon retires in bad-tempered impatience, completely unable to cope with these living problems from a world with which he is unfamiliar; but Escalus is more tolerant. He speaks to Pompey and Elbow in their own language and joins in their cross-talk, shooing off Froth with a witty warning, and drawing from Pompey some observations that must confound all would-be sexual legislators. Unless they are prepared to 'geld and splay all the youth of the city', then, in Pompey's opinion, 'they will to't'.

Escalus has no answer. Turning his attention to Elbow and tactfully praising him for his 'readiness in office' (but evidently determined that he shall not continue in it), he gives a final sigh for Claudio—and goes off to dinner.

Scene 2 Even the kindly provost has taken it upon himself to check that Angelo really intends to execute Claudio, and has had no second thoughts. Angelo is adamant, and when asked about 'the groaning Juliet', dismisses her as 'the fornicatress'.

Isabella's first, tentative, approaches to this unbending power figure are watched by the sympathetic provost ('Heaven give thee moving graces'), and stage-managed by Lucio—'Kneel down before him, hang upon his gown . . . '. A second assay engages Angelo in a dialogue, and Isabella, although the supplicant, is immediately in control of the argument. Angelo cannot move from the position he first adopted, and his statement of that position ('Look what I will not, that I cannot do') declares its weakness, giving the impression that Claudio's fate is not so much a matter of law as of Angelo's personal will. Further encouragement ('You are too cold') from Lucio spurs Isabella on to an appeal for mercy which, gathering strength in eloquence, becomes a dynamic confrontation of two absolutes that counter and challenge each other's argument. The old law confronts the new testament: justice encounters mercy, and power is defied by weakness. Angelo stands firm on his legal position—but Isabella (with whispered applause, aside, from Lucio and the provost) invokes the teaching of Christianity. For Angelo, Claudio's life is 'a forfeit of the law', but Isabella believes that 'all the souls that were'—i.e. the whole of humankind—were once condemned under God's law, but have been redeemed through God's mercy. As Escalus had done, she turns the question back on Angelo

> Go to your bosom,
> Knock there, and ask your heart what it doth know
> That's like my brother's fault.

—and momentarily he is at a loss. A loophole seems to be offered when Isabella suggests that she might 'bribe' him, but this is no escape. Angelo, defeated, postpones further confrontation until the following day.

Isabella's questions have struck home through Angelo's icy armour, forcing him to admit a new and appalling sensation—lust. He stumbles in a moral and emotional maze, where carrion flesh corrupts in sunshine, and nameless evils defile the ruined sanctuary.

Scene 3 The duke also seems to learn something new when, disguised as a prison-visiting friar, he encounters the pregnant Juliet. She is sorry for what she has done—but only because it is considered unlawful—and she rejoices in her pregnancy, her 'shame'. The duke's preaching is superfluous, and his parting words are cruel—'Your partner, as I hear, must die tomorrow'.

Scene 4 'Tomorrow' is already here for the tormented Angelo, forced now to admit that 'blood'—natural sexual desire—is stronger than all the statecraft he has studied and the 'gravity' of which he is so proud. Isabella's renewed plea for Claudio's life is met with riddling suggestiveness and hypothetical disputation to which the nun—although she fails to understand its direction—responds with eager passion and imagery that stirs Angelo's blood to spell out further propositions. Shame and self-disgust manifest themselves equally with lust and cruelty in his demands as his tongue relishes the thought of the 'sweet uncleanness' and the 'treasures' of Isabella's chaste body.

At first Isabella's innocence cannot comprehend the extent of Angelo's depravity. In some kind of martyrdom she would willingly lay down her life for her brother, but her strict, self-imposed chastity will not hear of anything less absolute. The final assault of Angelo's rhetoric turns her own words back against her. Having defined women as creatures who are essentially frail, Isabella lays herself open to Angelo's challenge—

> Be that you are,
> That is, a woman; if you be more, you're none.
> If you be one . . .
> . . . show it now
> By putting on the destin'd livery.

At last Isabella realizes what is required of her, and her shocked horror reaches for its only remaining weapon: 'I will proclaim thee, Angelo . . . I'll tell the world aloud What man thou art'. But her threats meet with the bland assurance of the rapist's security—'Who will believe thee, Isabel?'

With nothing now to lose, Angelo abandons argument and persuasion for menace and ultimatum, blocking any escape with the sure rhyme of his final couplet—

> As for you,
> Say what you can, my false o'erweighs your true.

Isabella is left to confront her own dilemma. Trusting that her brother's sense of honour will support her, she declares her decision in another couplet—but here the rhyme sounds far too easy:

> Then Isabel live chaste, and brother die:
> More than our brother is our chastity.

Act 3

Scene 1 Before Claudio can give an opinion, he must listen to some Stoic advice from the disguised duke. Life—what's it worth? You're no longer young, and when you get older you'll only be a burden to yourself and your family . . . Claudio replies politely, responding rather to such Christian consolation as he might expect from a friar than to anything he is hearing now. As he turns to his sister, he is still hoping for some 'remedy'.

Standing aside with the provost, but still in view of the audience, the duke can be seen to overhear everything that passes between Isabella and her brother. With forced gaiety Isabella speaks of honour and endurance, and Claudio is initially prepared to be gallant and 'encounter darkness as a bride'—but is there no way out? When he hears of Angelo's proposition, which Isabella describes with embarrassment and abhorrence, he is at first outraged, then amazed—and then he begins to question the very nature of the crime for which he is condemned and which his judge is now proposing to commit: 'Sure it is no sin Or of the deadly seven it is the least'.

Thoughts of life and death inspire Claudio with an answer to the philosophical duke, and his vision of possible existences beyond this life are thrilling in their intensity—and terrifying to Isabella in their conclusion that 'The weariest and most loathed earthly life . . . is a paradise To what we fear of death'. The idealistic Isabella cannot rise to her brother's challenge now, and she abuses Claudio with a violence that seems to spring more from sexual horror than from concern with family honour.

The heated emotions are cooled (and the poetry changes to prose) when the 'friar' offers a clumsy (and cruel) excuse for Angelo's intentions—then proves himself unexpectedly resourceful! Shakespeare, to protect his chaste heroine, has introduced into his source story an old device, the 'bed trick', and a new character, Mariana—formerly betrothed to Angelo but deserted by him when her dowry failed to materialize. The substitute bride in the unknowing husband's bed was a familiar ploy used by story-tellers, and Isabella is easily persuaded to agree that Mariana should take her place in an assignation with the corrupt deputy. Happily, she goes off to make the necessary arrangements—and the 'friar' remains on stage to listen to Elbow's argument with his prisoner, the unrepentant Pompey.

Scene 2 Pompey has been arrested for pimping, and although he can still joke with the constable, he is reduced to silence by the reproaches of the duke, who is shocked to learn that a man should earn his living from such a 'filthy vice'. But Mistress Overdone and her trade are declining, and Pompey's final appeal is even rejected by Lucio, who has suddenly become greasily self-righteous, eager to ingratiate himself with the 'friar' and impress him with a display of inside information.

Lucio is shrewd and inventive in his assessment of Angelo ('Some report a sea-maid spawned him'), and he seems to have an uncanny grasp of the situation when he says that the duke has 'usurp[ed] the beggary he was never born to'. But he cannot penetrate the duke's disguise, and his crude scandals provoke the 'friar' to defend his own reputation with a promise to 'call upon' Lucio to maintain these fantasies at some future date. Lucio takes his leave cheerfully enough, but Mistress Overdone, arrested as a 'bawd of eleven years continuance', now supplies additional evidence against him with her information that for fifteen months she has been caring for his illegitimate child, the offspring of yet another broken engagement!

The duke, whose disguise has allowed him to enter into the lowest depths of the society that he should govern, now meditates (in rhymed octosyllabics) on the qualities needed in an ideal ruler—and this meditation provides the turning-point of the play.

Act 4

Scene 1 Mariana, who is still desolated by Angelo's rejection of her, welcomes the duke's proposal to trick him, her husband 'on a pre-contract', into a relationship that will be almost parallel to that of Claudio and Juliet.

Scene 2 In a short episode of black comedy, Pompey exchanges his prison fetters for an executioner's axe—and Shakespeare introduces the name of Barnardine, another character of his own creation who is necessary for his new treatment of an old plot.

It is now 'dead midnight', and throughout this scene we are always conscious of the passing time as we wait with the provost and the disguised duke in hope of a last-minute reprieve for Claudio. Tension mounts with every knock on the door, but the duke seems confident, until the moment when the letter is opened and read aloud, that Angelo will honour his promise. But what Angelo believed to have been the sacrifice of Isabella's virginity has only intensified his determination to execute her brother. The duke must make a rapid change of plan, and the existence of Barnardine, 'one that is a prisoner nine years old', seems to offer an instant solution: Barnardine can have 'a present shrift', and his head instead of Claudio's can be presented to Angelo.

Having convinced the provost of his special authority, the 'friar' takes charge of the situation. It is 'almost clear dawn', and a pastoral peace seems assured as 'th'unfolding star calls up the shepherd'—

Scene 3 —but it is not daylight yet, although Pompey is enjoying his little jokes with Barnardine, his intended victim. Life, it would seem, cannot be engineered as the duke would have it: Barnardine hasn't the slightest intention of dying to satisfy anybody's convenience, and even a drunken murderer cannot be judicially executed without proper preparation. A lucky chance ('an accident that heaven provides') allows the duke to wriggle out of this very tricky situation—until Isabella appears!

For the purposes of the plot, Isabella must not be told that her brother is still alive, and the 'friar' offers a clumsy pretext of some spiritual exercise. But if Isabella will follow his instructions, he promises, she can be revenged on Angelo: the duke has changed his plans, and will be back in Vienna the next day—although the 'friar' himself has suddenly been called away. Isabella is all meekness—but as she is leaving the stage her path is crossed by the unexpected and unwelcome appearance of Lucio.

Although grieving for Claudio, and frightened for himself, Lucio is still able to reminisce with his falsehoods about 'the old fantastical duke of dark corners', and to boast of a lucky escape from Angelo's sentence. But the audience knows that Lucio's luck is running out . . .

Scene 4 The duke's 'letters of strange tenor' are perplexing to Angelo, whose mind is already in turmoil and acutely sensitive now to Isabella's 'tender shame' and her 'maiden loss'. The 'blood' that would not be denied (2, 4, 15) has betrayed him: his first crime led him, inexorably, to the second, and both weigh heavily on his conscience.

Scene 5 More letters—more instructions. Friar Peter, it seems, has been taken into the duke's confidence, and the whole of Vienna is being alerted.

Scene 6 Isabella and Mariana have also been instructed about the parts they are to play in the duke's little charade—and the audience is brought into the secret: Isabella must allow Angelo to continue in his belief that he has raped her, even though the 'friar' may contradict her. It is much against her will—but ''tis a physic That's bitter to sweet end'.

The scene is set: the characters are ready and waiting . . .

Act 5

Scene 1 The day of reckoning! That same duke who had declared 'I do not like to stage me to [the people's] eyes' (*1*, 1, 68) will now take not one but *two* major roles in a production of his own devising. The theatre audience can guess the outcome—but how will this be achieved?

After an impressive entrance—flanked on either side by Angelo and Escalus, and looking like an icon of Justice—the duke listens sympathetically to Isabella's eloquent appeal. He intends a long, slow exposure of his deputy, giving Angelo every opportunity to tighten the noose around his own neck, and he steers Isabella (despite Lucio's ill-timed interruption) in the direction he would have her go until she is able to accuse Angelo of 'concupiscible intemperate lust'.

This the duke cannot believe! It is impossible—Angelo's integrity is 'without blemish'—and it is unreasonable:

> If he had so offended,
> He would have weigh'd thy brother by himself
> And not have cut him off.

This is what Angelo had predicted (2, 4, 155–6), and the guilty deputy can relax into false security when Isabella is removed from the scene and Friar Peter's testimony is heard, utterly discrediting Isabella, and declaring Angelo to be completely 'free from touch or soil with her'. And there is another witness to be called in Angelo's defence (although 'Friar Lodowick' is temporarily indisposed).

'Do you not smile at this, Lord Angelo?': the duke extends an invitation for Angelo to sit and watch the performance as Friar Peter brings in the veiled Mariana with her riddling 'I have known my husband, yet my husband Knows not that ever he knew me'. Lucio's intrusions are irritating for the duke—but they prolong the audience's delighted anticipation of the coming denouement. Angelo is not unduly disturbed when Mariana reveals herself, and he admits to the broken engagement—though not (understandably) to the clandestine intercourse. With breathtaking impudence he offers to take charge of the proceedings, and the duke, setting Escalus in his place, vanishes without further explanation.

Ironies multiply furiously when the officers go to seek 'Friar Lodowick' and the duke, reassuming his religious habit, returns to the trial. Pretending sympathy for Mariana and Isabella (also returned to the stage), the 'friar' warns them that without the duke there will be no justice in Vienna—a city where he has seen corruption 'boil and bubble Till it o'errun the stew'. Escalus interprets this as slander to the state and, encouraged by Lucio (who attributes to the 'friar' all his own defamatory remarks about the duke), he orders the 'friar' to be arrested. Lucio lends a hand in carrying out his command—and pulls off the hood that disguises the duke!

Totally devastated, Angelo craves instant death—but he is first sentenced to be married to the woman he has wronged. Whilst this ceremony is being performed the duke tries to make some excuses to Isabella, asking her to pardon, for Mariana's sake, Angelo's intentions against her chastity. Whatever Isabella's thoughts may be now, they are well concealed by her submissive words!

Now the newly-married Angelo waits for the duke's verdict on his first crime, perhaps remembering his own self-righteous reply to Escalus's plea for mercy—

> When I that censure him do so offend
> Let mine own judgement pattern out my death
>
> (2, 1, 29–30)

The duke would seem to be in agreement with this principle—a death for a death, an Angelo for a Claudio—but he has Mariana to reckon with! Desperate to save her husband, she begs for Isabella's eloquence to aid her cause when the duke reiterates his judgement:

> He dies for Claudio's death.

The stage now belongs to the actress playing Isabella, revolving in her mind the memory of her appeals to Angelo, his rejections of them, her brother's anguished pleadings and his visionary horror of death, her bitter disappointment when promises were broken, the suddenness of the execution . . . In the theatre this moment never fails! Whatever the audience, and no matter how many times its members have seen/heard/read the play, the force of Shakespeare's verse wipes out all thoughts but—'Will Isabella kneel down?'

A long silence (the greater the actress, the longer the silence), then a sigh of relief.

But the duke remembers the haste of Claudio's execution, and questions the provost about this irregularity, still holding Angelo in suspense and prolonging his public embarrassment. Escalus adds his reproaches, disappointed that 'one so learned and wise' should 'slip so grossly', and the mortified Angelo, utterly destroyed in his own self-esteem, would rather have death than any show of mercy.

The provost brings in his prisoners, Barnardine and a 'muffled fellow', and the duke hurries the play towards its conclusion. When Claudio is discovered, Angelo is reprieved: Isabella has her brother, and Mariana her husband—but any surprise or relief, joy or gratitude, must be expressed speechlessly. The duke has a request to make—but, again, there are no words, no time, for Isabella's answer—and there is one other matter to deal with.

Lucio, and the slanderous abuses that have so often enlivened proceedings for the audience, must be punished—if not with the threatened whipping and hanging, then at least by marriage with the prostitute whose child is being cared for by Mistress Overdone. Lucio is allowed one last quip—'Marrying a punk, my lord, is pressing to death, whipping, and hanging'—but the duke has a ready return: 'Slandering a prince deserves it'. Perhaps there would have been special applause from the royal spectator at one of the play's earliest performances: James I

(James VI of Scotland) was well-known for his sensitivity to slander—which since 1585 had been a treasonable offence in Scotland, punishable by death.

All are finally reconciled in a general prizegiving, and rhyming couplets bring the play to a hasty but tidy end. The duke has a proposition for Isabella—

> Whereto, if you'll a willing ear incline,
> What's mine is yours, and what is yours is mine

—but Isabella can make no reply. Interpretation of her response is open for every actress, director—and reader.

Measure for Measure and the art of Tragicomedy

'It is a *hateful* work . . . [and] our feelings of justice are grossly wounded in Angelo's escape'

(Samuel Taylor Coleridge)

The ending of *Measure for Measure* has disappointed many readers—although few have expressed their feelings quite so vehemently as the poet Coleridge. The four characters (Angelo and Isabella, Claudio and—to a less degree—Mariana) with whom the readers have been so intimately involved have all just experienced surprising reversals of fortune and now suddenly—they have nothing to say for themselves! Without comment they accept all the disclosures and couplings engineered by the duke—including his proposal of marriage to the would-be nun who, less than a week ago, had wanted further restrictions on the order of the 'Poor Clares'. The emotions of readers, once aroused, are not so easily satisfied, and the play is seen to deserve the label 'Problem Play'.

But in the theatre—it's a different matter. Feelings are just as powerfully stirred by the authenticity of the characters and their tragic potential, but audiences are always aware of the omnipresent duke—who is easily overlooked in a reading of the play. From his first interview with Friar Thomas it is clear that the duke will be in control of the situation, and the audience can watch his well-plotted action in a *comfortable* suspense, confident of a happy ending for everybody. Claudio will not be executed: there may be danger, but there will be no death.

This is the very essence of *tragicomedy*, the latest trend in drama (where fashions changed almost as quickly as fashions in clothes) when Shakespeare was writing *Measure for Measure*. The new form had been introduced into England from Italy, and soon became even more popular than the traditional forms of tragedy and comedy.

According to the classical literary theory that still held sway throughout Europe, tragedy demanded great actions and noble personages; its proper medium was verse, and its language should be appropriately exalted. Comedy, on the other hand, should deal with everyday affairs in normal, matter-of-fact speech, and concern itself only with characters from the lower social classes. Tragedy heads directly for disaster and, usually, death; comedy takes a roundabout way to a happy ending with, most probably, marriage as its climax. Tragicomedy, whose characters are neither noble nor humble, is a prolonged flirtation with danger without any real risk—an extended tightrope-walking with many false steps and hesitations but with a secure safety-net. It is a certain recipe for popular entertainment in many forms and media—especially television! Whatever serious issues are raised in tragicomedy, they are never seriously debated and pursued to their logical conclusions. Repentance and forgiveness matter more than justice and revenge, and the frustration of wrongdoing is more important than its punishment: Angelo's criminal abuse of his power is in intention only, and the plot of the play will never allow him to become the out-and-out villain of the piece—any more than Isabella can become its flawless heroine.

Apart from the duke, the characters in *Measure for Measure* are all ordinary people, of moderate means and understanding and, like Barnardine, 'desperately mortal' (4, 2, 136). Only divine providence in the person of the duke can protect them from their own extremes of wickedness and virtue—and even this providential duke needs some assistance from the playwright when a severed head is called for! Duke Vincentio is no celestial manifestation, a god come down from heaven, and no allegorical representation of Justice or Mercy. Although he belongs to a long tradition of disguised fictional onlookers—gods, angels, kings, and even civil authorities—who survey the landscape of human activity and criticize its shortcomings, he is nevertheless a character in his own right, and, like all the other characters, open to criticism as well as interpretation.

Shakespeare's Verse

Easily the best way to understand and appreciate Shakespeare's verse is to read it aloud—and don't worry if you don't understand everything! Try not to be captivated by the dominant rhythm, but decide which are the most important words in each line and use the regular metre to drive them forward to the listeners.

Shakespeare's plays are written mainly in blank verse, the form preferred by most dramatists in the sixteenth and early seventeenth centuries. It is a very flexible medium, capable—like the human speaking voice—of a wide range of tones. Basically the lines, called 'iambic pentameters', are unrhymed and have ten syllables with alternating stresses (just like normal English speech) which divide them into five 'feet'. The rhythm of the pentameter is initiated for *Measure for Measure* in the first scene of the play when the duke is delegating his authority to Angelo in the presence of Escalus. It is a very formal occasion, and the verse is appropriately correct:

Duke

Of góvernmént the própertiés to unfóld
Would séem in mé t'afféct speech ánd discóurse,
Since Í am pút to knów that yóur own scíence
Excéeds, in thát, the lísts of áll advíce
My stréngth can gíve you. Thén no móre remáins
But thát, to yóur suffíciency, ás your wórth is áble,
And lét them wórk. The náture óf our péople,
Our cíty's ínstitútions, ánd the térms
For cómmon jústice, y'áre as prégnant ín
As árt and práctice háth enríchèd ány
That wé remémber.

At the beginning of his career Shakespeare wrote regular, 'end-stopped' lines in which the unit of meaning was contained within the pentameter, but such lines ('In our remove be thou at full ourself', line 43) are rare in *Measure for Measure.* Here the sense runs freely between the lines, usually with a strong mid-line pause (a 'caesura') for added control and emphasis (which is especially necessary for the heated emotions in Isabella's arguments with Angelo—*Act 2*, Scenes 2 and 4). The length of the lines may now be longer or shorter than the basic ten syllables of Shakespeare's early pentameters and sometimes, as in ordinary speech, syllables are elided ('t'affect', 'y'are', 'th'observer'), but the rhythm is never lost, even when a line is shared between two or more speakers:

Escalus
If ány ín Viénna bé of wórth
To úndergó such ámple gráce and hónour
It ís Lord Ángeló.

Enter Angelo

Duke
Look whére he cómes.

Angelo
Alwáys obédient tó your gráce's wíll
I cóme to knów your pléasure.

Duke
Ángeló:
There ís a kínd of cháracter ín thy lífe
That tó th'obsérver dóth thy hístory
Fúlly unfóld.

Source, Date, and Text

There are many versions of this story of the corrupt magistrate, but Shakespeare's starting point for *Measure for Measure* was probably an earlier play, *Promos and Cassandra* by George Whetstone. This was published in 1578 (but never performed) and tells how the virtuous Cassandra tries to save the life of her brother Andrugio, condemned to death for adultery by the severe judge Promos.

Promos demands Cassandra's virginity as the price of her brother's life and the girl, under pressure from Andrugio, is forced to consent. When Cassandra has fulfilled her part of the bargain, however, Promos orders the jailer to present her with her brother's head—but the sympathetic jailer (who is disgusted by the 'lewdness' of Promos) is able to substitute the head of a recently executed felon, 'by the providence of God provided thus for his safety'. Cassandra appeals to the king for vengeance on Promos, and the king sentences him to be first married to Cassandra and then put to death. When the marriage has been solemnized, Cassandra finds herself 'tied in the greatest bonds of affection to her husband', and she pleads most earnestly for his life. The king refuses to grant her petition—but the disguised Andrugio reveals his identity, and Promos is pardoned.

Shakespeare treats this story even more seriously than the moralistic Whetstone: his heroine is not merely virtuous but devoutly vowed—almost—to chastity. With the introduction of Mariana and the traditional device of the 'bed trick'—the substituted bride in the unknowing husband's bed—Shakespeare makes it possible for Isabella to keep her virginity and to be able to plead for Angelo's life without having to marry him. Instead of Whetstone's king, who is brought in only at the last minute to rescue an otherwise insoluble situation, Shakespeare's duke is present from the very first scene. He is one of many disguised rulers in plays written around the time of *Measure for Measure* who roamed around their cities to spy out and remedy the abuses of those in power.

Measure for Measure was performed at court before King James on 26 December 1604, and was probably written earlier that year. The description of subjects crowding in upon their monarch (2, 4, 27–30) may refer to an incident in March 1604 when the king visited the Royal Exchange, hoping to watch the merchants unobserved; news of the visit leaked out, and the doors had to be closed against the throngs pressing in to see him.

The play was not published until 1623, and the text shows some signs of having been censored under an Act of 1606 which imposed harsh penalties for the improper use of the name of God (see 2, 4, 4–5). The present edition is based on the text established by Brian Gibbons for the New Cambridge Shakespeare (Cambridge, 1991).

People in the Play

Vincentio	*Duke of Vienna*
Angelo	*The* duke's *deputy*
Escalus	*an ancient lord*
Claudio	*a young gentleman*
Lucio	Claudio*'s friend*
Provost	*marshal in charge of the prison*
Elbow	*a simple constable*
Abhorson	*an executioner*
Justice	*assistant to* Escalus
Froth	*a foolish gentleman*
Pompey	*a pimp and tapster*
Barnardine	*a condemned murderer*
Friar Thomas **Friar Peter**	*Franciscan friars*
Two Gentlemen	
Isabella	Claudio*'s sister, a novice nun*
Juliet	Claudio*'s sweetheart*
Mariana	*formerly betrothed to* Angelo
Mistress Overdone	*a bawd*
Francisca	*a sister of the Order of St Clare*

Lords, Officers, Servants, Citizens, a Boy

The action of the play takes place in Vienna and in Mariana's country house

'If any in Vienna be of worth To undergo such ample grace and honour It is Lord Angelo.' (*1*, 1, 22–4) Stephen Boxer as Angelo, Royal Shakespeare Company, 1998.

ACT 1

Act 1 Scene 1
The Duke of Vienna delegates his authority to Angelo.

SCENE 1

The Duke*'s office: enter* Duke, Escalus, Lords

Duke
Escalus.

Escalus
My lord.

Duke
Of government the properties to unfold
Would seem in me t'affect speech and discourse,
Since I am put to know that your own science
Exceeds, in that, the lists of all advice
My strength can give you. Then no more remains
But that, to your sufficiency, as your worth is able,
And let them work. The nature of our people,
Our city's institutions, and the terms
For common justice, y'are as pregnant in
As art and practice hath enriched any
That we remember. There is our commission,
From which we would not have you warp. Call hither,
I say, bid come before us Angelo. [*Exit a* Lord
What figure of us think you he will bear?
For you must know, we have with special soul
Elected him our absence to supply,
Lent him our terror, dress'd him with our love,
And given his deputation all the organs
Of our own power. What think you of it?

Escalus
If any in Vienna be of worth
To undergo such ample grace and honour
It is Lord Angelo.

Enter Angelo

3 *properties*: essential qualities.
unfold: explain, enlarge upon.
4 *affect . . . discourse*: enjoy hearing myself talk.
5 *put to know*: forced to recognize.
science: specialist knowledge.
6 *lists*: limits.
7 *strength*: intellectual power (*and also*, ducal authority).
7–9 *no more . . . work*: no more remains for your complete authority but to add my strength to your governmental skills, as well as you can, and let them work together.
8 *sufficiency*: authority.
worth: virtue, moral integrity.
10 *institutions*: legal system (so called from the *Institutions*, a treatise on Roman law by Justinian).
10–11 *terms . . . justice*: conditions of the administration of justice.
11 *pregnant in*: well-informed about, quick in apprehension of.
12 *enriched*: enrichèd.
13 *commission*: warrant; the duke probably hands Escalus a document.
14 *warp*: deviate, swerve.
16 *What . . . bear*: what do you think he will be like as my representative.
17 *with special soul*: with absolute confidence.
18 *Elected*: chosen.
supply: fill as substitute.
19 *Lent*: The stress on this word insists that Angelo's power is merely provisional.
terror: power to command respect.
our love: i.e. the duke's love for his people, and theirs for him.
20 *deputation*: office of deputy.
organs: instruments.
23 *undergo*: bear the weight of.

27 *character*: sign, handwriting.
28 *th'observer*: anyone who looks.
29 *belongings*: gifts, capabilities.
30 *thine . . . proper*: exclusively your own property.
waste: indulge.
31 *virtues*: talents.
32–3 *Heaven . . . themselves*: 'Neither do men light a candle, and put it under a bushel, but on a candlestick, and it giveth light unto all that are in the house' (Matthew 5:15).
33–6 *our virtues . . . issues*: The duke seems to allude to the story of the woman who was cured of 'an issue of blood' by touching the garment worn by Jesus—who 'did know in himself the virtue that went out of him'.
35–6 *Spirits . . . issues*: our spirits are only moved to great emotions for great purposes. The duke uses the image of gold coins, officially tested with the touchstone, and issued as current and valuable.
37 *scruple*: the smallest unit of weight.
38–9 *determines . . . creditor*: makes sure she has the glory due to a creditor.
40 *use*: interest.
bend: address.
41 *my part in him*: the role of governor that I have lent to him.
advertise: inform, give instruction to.
42 *Hold therefore*: keep on like that.
43 *remove*: absence.
at full: in every respect.
44 *Mortality*: authority to pronounce sentence of death.
46 *in question*: appointed.
secondary: second-in-command.
48 *metal*: Making a pun on 'mettle' (= spirit, courage), Angelo takes up the duke's image from lines 35–6.
49–50 *so noble . . . upon it*: English gold coins were stamped with either an image of the monarch, or a device of the archangel Michael—and known as 'nobles', or 'angels'.

Duke
Look where he comes.

Angelo
Always obedient to your grace's will
I come to know your pleasure.

Duke
Angelo:
There is a kind of character in thy life
That to th'observer doth thy history
Fully unfold. Thyself and thy belongings
Are not thine own so proper as to waste
Thyself upon thy virtues, they on thee.
Heaven doth with us as we with torches do,
Not light them for themselves: for if our virtues
Did not go forth of us, 'twere all alike
As if we had them not. Spirits are not finely touch'd
But to fine issues: nor nature never lends
The smallest scruple of her excellence
But, like a thrifty goddess, she determines
Herself the glory of a creditor,
Both thanks and use. But I do bend my speech
To one that can my part in him advertise.
Hold therefore, Angelo:
In our remove be thou at full ourself.
Mortality and mercy in Vienna
Live in thy tongue and heart. Old Escalus,
Though first in question, is thy secondary.
Take thy commission.

Angelo
Now good my lord,
Let there be some more test made of my metal
Before so noble and so great a figure
Be stamp'd upon it.

Duke

No more evasion.
We have with a leaven'd and prepared choice
Proceeded to you; therefore take your honours.
Our haste from hence is of so quick condition
That it prefers itself and leaves unquestion'd
Matters of needful value. We shall write to you,
As time and our concernings shall importune,
How it goes with us, and do look to know
What doth befall you here. So fare you well.
To th'hopeful execution do I leave you
Of your commissions.

Angelo

Yet give leave, my lord,
That we may bring you something on the way.

Duke

My haste may not admit it,
Nor need you, on mine honour, have to do
With any scruple. Your scope is as mine own
So to enforce or qualify the laws
As to your soul seems good. Give me your hand,
I'll privily away. I love the people,
But do not like to stage me to their eyes:
Though it do well I do not relish well
Their loud applause and aves vehement,
Nor do I think the man of safe discretion
That does affect it. Once more, fare you well.

Angelo

The heavens give safety to your purposes.

Escalus

Lead forth and bring you back in happiness.

Duke

I thank you, fare you well. [*Exit*

Escalus

I shall desire you, sir, to give me leave
To have free speech with you; and it concerns me
To look into the bottom of my place.
A power I have, but of what strength and nature
I am not yet instructed.

51 *leaven'd and prepared*: preparèd; very carefully considered: in bread-making, the dough must be prepared for baking by being 'leavened' with yeast to make it rise.

53 *quick*: urgent.

54 *prefers*: gives priority to. *unquestion'd*: undiscussed.

55 *of needful value*: that needed attention.

59 *execution*: performance.

61 *bring . . . way*: accompany you for part of the way.

63–4 *have . . . scruple*: have the least hesitation about this.

64 *scope*: freedom to act.

67 *privily*: secretly.

68 *stage me*: make a public exhibition of myself.

69 *do well*: succeed (i.e. as a performance, or as public relations strategy).

70 *aves*: acclamations (Latin *ave* = hail).

78 *look . . . place*: find out the full extent.

Angelo
'Tis so with me. Let us withdraw together
And we may soon our satisfaction have
Touching that point.

Escalus
I'll wait upon your honour.

[*Exeunt*

83 *wait upon*: attend.

Scene 2

Act 1 Scene 2
Lucio and his friends meet Mistress Overdone and learn that Claudio has been condemned to death by Angelo. Claudio needs help from his sister, and sends Lucio with a message.

A street in Vienna: enter Lucio, *and two other* Gentlemen

Lucio
If the duke, with the other dukes, come not to composition with the king of Hungary, why then all the dukes fall upon the king.

First Gentleman
Heaven grant us its peace, but not the king of Hungary's.

Second Gentleman
Amen.

Lucio
Thou conclud'st like the sanctimonious pirate that went to sea with the ten commandments, but scraped one out of the table.

Second Gentleman
Thou shalt not steal?

2 *composition*: agreement.
9 *table*: tablet; the Ten Commandments were displayed on tablets of wood or stone in English churches.

11 *razed*: erased.

13 *functions*: callings, occupations.

18 *grace*: the thanksgiving before meat.

22 *proportion*: metrical rhythm.
24 *Grace*: the mercy and love of God.
27 *there . . . us*: we're both made of the same stuff.
28 *lists*: selvages, the edges of a piece of cloth.

31 *three-piled*: triple-napped.
had as lief: would rather.
32 *kersey*: coarse woollen cloth.
piled: a) bald; b) suffering from piles (haemorrhoids). Both these were associated with syphilis, a sexually transmitted condition popularly known as 'the French disease'.
33 *feelingly*: to the point.
36 *begin*: drink to.
36–7 *drink after thee*: i.e. for fear of infection.

Lucio
Ay, that he razed.

First Gentleman
Why, 'twas a commandment to command the captain and all the rest from their functions: they put forth to steal. There's not a soldier of us all that, in the thanksgiving before meat, do relish the petition well that prays for peace.

Second Gentleman
I never heard any soldier dislike it.

Lucio
I believe thee, for I think thou never wast where grace was said.

Second Gentleman
No? A dozen times at least.

First Gentleman
What? In metre?

Lucio
In any proportion, or in any language.

First Gentleman
I think, or in any religion.

Lucio
Ay? Why not? Grace is grace, despite of all controversy: as, for example, thou thyself art a wicked villain, despite of all grace.

First Gentleman
Well, there went but a pair of shears between us.

Lucio
I grant: as there may between the lists and the velvet. Thou art the list.

First Gentleman
And thou the velvet. Thou art good velvet: thou'rt a three-piled piece, I warrant thee. I had as lief be a list of an English kersey as be piled, as thou art piled, for a French velvet. Do I speak feelingly now?

Lucio
I think thou dost, and indeed with most painful feeling of thy speech. I will, out of thine own confession, learn to begin thy health; but, whilst I live, forget to drink after thee.

First Gentleman
I think I have done myself wrong, have I not?

Second Gentleman
Yes, that thou hast, whether thou art tainted or free.

Enter Mistress Overdone, *a Bawd*

Lucio
Behold, behold, where Madam Mitigation comes. I have purchased as many diseases under her roof as come to—

Second Gentleman
To what, I pray?

Lucio
Judge.

Second Gentleman
To three thousand dolours a year.

First Gentleman
Ay, and more.

Lucio
A French crown more.

First Gentleman
Thou art always figuring diseases in me, but thou art full of error: I am sound.

Lucio
Nay, not, as one would say, healthy, but so sound as things that are hollow. Thy bones are hollow. Impiety has made a feast of thee.

First Gentleman
How now, which of your hips has the most profound sciatica?

Mistress Overdone
Well, well: there's one yonder arrested and carried to prison was worth five thousand of you all.

Second Gentleman
Who's that, I pray thee?

Mistress Overdone
Marry, sir, that's Claudio, Signior Claudio.

First Gentleman
Claudio to prison? 'Tis not so.

38 *done . . . wrong*: let myself be beaten.

39 *tainted*: infected.

40 *Madam Mitigation*: the lady of (sexual) satisfaction.

44 *dolours*: diseases (with a pun on 'dollars').

46 *French crown*: a) a coin; b) a bald head (a symptom of 'the French disease').

49–50 *so sound . . . hollow*: i.e. resonant ('sound as a bell').

50 *bones . . . hollow*: i.e. with osteoporosis (a symptom of secondary and tertiary syphilis).

52 *profound*: deep-seated.

53 *sciatica*: This was also thought to be a symptom of advanced syphilis.

54–85 *there's one yonder . . . man*: The contradictions and duplications in these lines suggest that Shakespeare has not revised his work!

57 *Marry*: By the Virgin Mary (a mild oath).

Mistress Overdone

Nay, but I know 'tis so. I saw him arrested, saw him carried away, and, which is more, within these three days his head to be chopped off!

Lucio

But, after all this fooling, I would not have it so. Art thou sure of this?

Mistress Overdone

I am too sure of it: and it is for getting Madam Julietta with child.

Lucio

Believe me, this may be. He promised to meet me two hours since, and he was ever precise in promise-keeping.

Second Gentleman

Besides, you know, it draws something near to the speech we had to such a purpose.

First Gentleman

But most of all agreeing with the proclamation.

Lucio

Away. Let's go learn the truth of it.

[*Exeunt* Lucio *and* Gentlemen

Mistress Overdone

Thus, what with the war, what with the sweat, what with the gallows, and what with poverty, I am custom-shrunk.

Enter Pompey

How now? What's the news with you?

Pompey

Yonder man is carried to prison.

Mistress Overdone

Well, what has he done?

Pompey

A woman.

Mistress Overdone

But what's his offence?

Pompey

Groping for trouts in a peculiar river.

70 *speech*: conversation.
to . . . purpose: on this subject.

73 *the sweat*: sweating sickness (a common form of plague).

81 *Groping . . . river*: catching trout (by tickling the underbellies) in a prohibited area—i.e. committing fornication.
peculiar: private, where fishing is not allowed.

Mistress Overdone

What? Is there a maid with child by him?

Pompey

No, but there's a woman with maid by him. You have not heard of the proclamation, have you?

Mistress Overdone

What proclamation, man?

Pompey

All houses in the suburbs of Vienna must be plucked down.

Mistress Overdone

And what shall become of those in the city?

Pompey

They shall stand for seed. They had gone down too, but that a wise burgher put in for them.

Mistress Overdone

But shall all our houses of resort in the suburbs be pulled down?

Pompey

To the ground, mistress.

Mistress Overdone

Why, here's a change indeed in the commonwealth. What shall become of me?

Pompey

Come, fear not you: good counsellors lack no clients. Though you change your place, you need not change your trade. I'll be your tapster still. Courage, there will be pity taken on you, you that have worn your eyes almost out in the service, you will be considered.

Mistress Overdone

What's to do here, Thomas Tapster? Let's withdraw.

Pompey

Here comes Signior Claudio, led by the provost to prison; and there's Madam Juliet. [*Exeunt*

Enter Provost, Claudio, Juliet, Officers, Lucio, *and two* Gentlemen

86 *houses*: brothels, houses of prostitution.
suburbs: built-up areas outside the city limits (and beyond the jurisdiction of the city authorities).

89 *stand for seed*: be left unharvested to provide seed for another season.

90 *put in*: made an offer.

94 *commonwealth*: state of the nation.

100 *service*: i.e. prostitution (the blind god Cupid was its patron).

Claudio
Fellow, why dost thou show me thus to th'world?
Bear me to prison, where I am committed.

Provost
I do it not in evil disposition,
But from Lord Angelo by special charge.

Claudio
Thus can the demi-god, Authority,
Make us pay down for our offence by weight
The words of heaven; on whom it will, it will,
On whom it will not, so; yet still 'tis just.

Lucio
Why, how now, Claudio? Whence comes this restraint?

Claudio
From too much liberty, my Lucio, liberty.
As surfeit is the father of much fast,
So every scope by the immoderate use
Turns to restraint. Our natures do pursue
Like rats that ravin down their proper bane
A thirsty evil, and when we drink, we die.

Lucio
If I could speak so wisely under an arrest, I would send for certain of my creditors; and yet, to say the truth, I had as lief have the foppery of freedom as the morality of imprisonment. What's thy offence, Claudio?

Claudio
What but to speak of would offend again.

Lucio
What, is't murder?

Claudio
No.

Lucio
Lechery?

Claudio
Call it so.

Provost
Away, sir, you must go.

Claudio
One word, good friend: Lucio, a word with you.

104 *show me . . . world*: Being exhibited in public was usually part of the criminal's punishment.

109–10 *pay down . . . heaven*: pay the full penalty ordained in the Bible for our offences (perhaps the retributive justice, 'an eye for an eye', of Exodus). Payment 'by weight' is more exact than payment by number of coins.

110–11 *on whom . . . so*: Claudio seems to accept the apparent arbitrariness of even divine justice: 'I will have mercy on whom I will have mercy' (Romans 9:15).

114 *surfeit*: excessive indulgence in food or drink.

115 *scope*: freedom.

117 *ravin*: ravenously devour.
proper bane: specific poison.

118 *thirsty*: causing thirst.

119–20 *I would . . . creditors*: i.e. to get himself arrested by them.

121 *foppery*: foolishness.
morality: moral instruction.

Lucio

A hundred, if they'll do you any good. Is lechery so looked after?

Claudio

Thus stands it with me. Upon a true contract
I got possession of Julietta's bed—
You know the lady, she is fast my wife,
Save that we do the denunciation lack
Of outward order. This we came not to
Only for propagation of a dower
Remaining in the coffer of her friends,
From whom we thought it meet to hide our love
Till time had made them for us. But it chances
The stealth of our most mutual entertainment
With character too gross is writ on Juliet.

Lucio

With child, perhaps?

Claudio

Unhappily, even so.
And the new deputy now for the duke—
Whether it be the fault and glimpse of newness,
Or whether that the body public be
A horse whereon the governor doth ride,
Who, newly in the seat, that it may know
He can command, lets it straight feel the spur;
Whether the tyranny be in his place,
Or in his eminence that fills it up,
I stagger in—but this new governor
Awakes me all the enrolled penalties
Which have, like unscour'd armour, hung by th'wall
So long that nineteen zodiacs have gone round
And none of them been worn; and for a name
Now puts the drowsy and neglected Act
Freshly on me: 'tis surely for a name.

Lucio

I warrant it is; and thy head stands so tickle on thy shoulders that a milkmaid, if she be in love, may sigh it off. Send after the duke and appeal to him.

Claudio

I have done so, but he's not to be found.
I prithee, Lucio, do me this kind service:

131 *looked after*: under surveillance.

132 *true contract*: proper betrothal.

134 *fast*: securely.

135–6 *denunciation . . . order*: official public declaration (as in the marriage ceremony).

137 *propagation*: increase, augmentation.
dower: dowry.

138 *friends*: i.e. relatives (whose approval, though not essential, was socially desirable).

140 *made . . . us*: won them over to our side.

142 *character too gross*: writing only too obvious.

145 *the fault . . . newness*: a mistake made in the uncertainty of the new position.

149 *straight*: immediately.

150 *in his place*: inherent in this office.

151 *his eminence . . . up*: the personal ambition of the man who holds it.

152 *stagger in*: am unable to decide, am uncertain.

153 *Awakes me*: goes and calls up; used in this way 'me' is merely emphatic.
enrolled: enrollèd; legally recorded.

154 *unscour'd*: unpolished.

155 *nineteen zodiacs*: The full cycle of the zodiac is completed in this period—but in *1*, 3, 22 the duke, more prosaically, refers to 'this fourteen years'.

156 *worn*: used (Claudio continues his metaphor from line 148).
name: reputation.

159 *I warrant*: I'm sure.
tickle: insecurely.

This day my sister should the cloister enter
And there receive her approbation.
Acquaint her with the danger of my state,
Implore her, in my voice, that she make friends
To the strict deputy: bid herself assay him.
I have great hope in that; for in her youth
There is a prone and speechless dialect
Such as move men; beside, she hath prosperous art
When she will play with reason and discourse,
And well she can persuade.

Lucio

I pray she may, as well for the encouragement of the like, which else would stand under grievous imposition, as for the enjoying of thy life, who I would be sorry should be thus foolishly lost at a game of tick-tack. I'll to her.

Claudio

I thank you, good friend Lucio.

Lucio

Within two hours.

Claudio

Come, officer, away. [*Exeunt*

165 *approbation*: probation, period as a novice.
168 *assay him*: test him out (i.e. like a coin—see *1*, 1, 35–6).
170 *a prone . . . dialect*: an eager way of speaking that doesn't need words.
171 *move*: The plural verb after the singular subject is apparently influenced by the two preceding adjectives.
prosperous: consistently successful.
172 *play . . . discourse*: enjoy argumentative discussion.
174–5 *the like*: others like yourself.
175 *stand . . . imposition*: be subject to some very serious charges.
177 *game of tick-tack*: A game in which pegs for scoring were driven into holes; a euphemism here for sexual intercourse.

Scene 3

Act 1 Scene 3
The duke confides in Friar Thomas.

The Friary: enter Duke *and* Friar Thomas

Duke

No. Holy father, throw away that thought,
Believe not that the dribbling dart of love
Can pierce a complete bosom. Why I desire thee
To give me secret harbour hath a purpose
More grave and wrinkled than the aims and ends
Of burning youth.

Friar

May your grace speak of it?

Duke

My holy sir, none better knows than you
How I have ever lov'd the life remov'd
And held in idle price to haunt assemblies

2 *dribbling dart*: feeble little arrow.
3 *complete*: impenetrable, without weakness (as though clad in complete armour).
5 *wrinkled*: given mature consideration.
9 *remov'd*: retired, withdrawn.

10 *held . . . price*: thought it not worthwhile.
11 *cost*: extravagance.
bravery: ostentation, display.
13 *stricture*: strict self-discipline.
15 *travell'd*: The Folio spelling 'travaild' shows that the stress here should be on the second syllable.
16 *strew'd . . . ear*: spread it about in public.
21 *weeds*: Shakespeare's imagery slides away from the expected 'steeds' as the duke becomes more vehement.
22 *this fourteen years*: See *1*, 2, 155note.
23 *o'er-grown . . . cave*: A classical story tells of an old lion who pretended to be sick and persuaded others to hunt and bring the prey back to his cave.
24 *fond*: foolish.
26 *it*: i.e. the birch twigs, the 'rod'.
29 *Dead . . . dead*: not having been enforced, might as well be dead.
30 *Liberty*: licentiousness, licence.
plucks . . . nose: An expression of utter contempt.
31 *athwart*: awry.
36 *Sith*: since.
37 *my tyranny*: tyranny in me.
42–4 *may . . . slander*: may strike to the heart of the matter under cover of my name, without bringing any disgrace on me personally.
44 *sway*: rule.

Where youth and cost witless bravery keeps.
I have deliver'd to Lord Angelo,
A man of stricture and firm abstinence,
My absolute power and place here in Vienna,
And he supposes me travell'd to Poland—
For so I have strew'd it in the common ear,
And so it is receiv'd. Now, pious sir,
You will demand of me why I do this.

Friar

Gladly, my lord.

Duke

We have strict statutes and most biting laws,
The needful bits and curbs to headstrong weeds,
Which for this fourteen years we have let slip,
Even like an o'er-grown lion in a cave
That goes not out to prey. Now, as fond fathers
Having bound up the threatening twigs of birch
Only to stick it in their children's sight
For terror, not to use—in time the rod
More mock'd than fear'd—so our decrees,
Dead to infliction, to themselves are dead,
And Liberty plucks Justice by the nose,
The baby beats the nurse, and quite athwart
Goes all decorum.

Friar

It rested in your grace
To unloose this tied-up justice when you pleas'd,
And it in you more dreadful would have seem'd
Than in Lord Angelo.

Duke

I do fear, too dreadful.
Sith 'twas my fault to give the people scope,
'Twould be my tyranny to strike and gall them
For what I bid them do: for we bid this be done
When evil deeds have their permissive pass
And not the punishment. Therefore indeed, my father,
I have on Angelo impos'd the office,
Who may in th'ambush of my name strike home,
And yet my nature never in the fight
To do in slander. And to behold his sway
I will, as 'twere a brother of your order,

Visit both prince and people. Therefore I prithee
Supply me with the habit, and instruct me
How I may formally in person bear
Like a true friar. Moe reasons for this action
At our more leisure shall I render you;
Only this one: Lord Angelo is precise,
Stands at a guard with envy, scarce confesses
That his blood flows, or that his appetite
Is more to bread than stone. Hence shall we see,
If power change purpose, what our seemers be.
[*Exeunt*

48 *formally*: in outward appearance and manner.
49 *Moe*: more.
51 *precise*: straitlaced, puritanical.
52 *Stands . . . envy*: is always on his guard against malice.

Act 1 Scene 4
Lucio tells Isabella of her brother's predicament.

Scene 4

The Convent of the Sisters of Saint Clare: enter Isabella *and* Francisca *a nun*

Isabella
And have you nuns no farther privileges?
Nun
Are not these large enough?

Isabella
Yes, truly; I speak not as desiring more,
But rather wishing a more strict restraint
Upon the sisterhood, the votarists of Saint Clare.

Lucio
[*Within*] Ho? Peace be in this place.

Isabella
Who's that which calls?

Nun
It is a man's voice. Gentle Isabella,
Turn you the key and know his business of him.
You may, I may not; you are yet unsworn:
When you have vow'd, you must not speak with men
But in the presence of the prioress;
Then if you speak you must not show your face,
Or if you show your face you must not speak.
He calls again: I pray you answer him. [*Stands aside*]

Isabella
Peace and prosperity. Who is't that calls?

Enter Lucio

Lucio
Hail virgin, if you be—as those cheek-roses
Proclaim you are no less—can you so stead me
As bring me to the sight of Isabella,
A novice of this place and the fair sister
To her unhappy brother Claudio?

Isabella
Why 'her unhappy brother'? Let me ask,
The rather for I now must make you know
I am that Isabella, and his sister.

Lucio
Gentle and fair: your brother kindly greets you.
Not to be weary with you, he's in prison.

Isabella
Woe me! For what?

Lucio
For that which, if myself might be his judge,
He should receive his punishment in thanks:
He hath got his friend with child.

5 *votarists . . . Saint Clare*: Sisters of the Order of Saint Clare (a strict Franciscan Order, popularly known as the 'Poor Clares').

17 *stead*: assist.

24 *kindly*: with brotherly affection.

25 *weary*: tedious, longwinded.

29 *friend*: lover.

30 *make . . . story*: don't give me any of your stories.

31 *familiar*: habitual.

32 *lapwing*: A bird well-known for deceiving predators by flying far away from its nest.

34 *enskied and sainted*: set like a saint in heaven.

38 *blaspheme . . . me*: blaspheme against the true saints by pretending that I am one of them.

39 *Fewness and truth*: briefly and honestly.

42–3 *from . . . foison*: brings the seed of a bare ploughed field ('fallow') to abundant harvest ('foison').

44 *Expresseth*: exhibits (by swelling out).
tilth: tilling.
husbandry: cultivation.

47 *change*: exchange.

48 *vain . . . affection*: affection natural enough ('apt') for their age but without meaning.

51–2 *Bore . . . hand*: led . . . to expect.

52 *action*: military action.

53 *nerves*: workings.

54 *His givings-out*: his public utterances.

Isabella
Sir, make me not your story.
Lucio
'Tis true.
I would not, though 'tis my familiar sin
With maids to seem the lapwing, and to jest
Tongue far from heart, play with all virgins so.
I hold you as a thing enskied and sainted,
By your renouncement an immortal spirit,
And to be talked with in sincerity
As with a saint.
Isabella
You do blaspheme the good in mocking me.
Lucio
Do not believe it. Fewness and truth, 'tis thus:
Your brother and his lover have embrac'd;
As those that feed grow full, as blossoming time
That from the seedness the bare fallow brings
To teeming foison, even so her plenteous womb
Expresseth his full tilth and husbandry.
Isabella
Someone with child by him? My cousin Juliet?
Lucio
Is she your cousin?
Isabella
Adoptedly, as schoolmaids change their names
By vain though apt affection.
Lucio
She it is.
Isabella
O, let him marry her.
Lucio
This is the point.
The duke is very strangely gone from hence;
Bore many gentlemen, myself being one,
In hand and hope of action: but we do learn,
By those that know the very nerves of state,
His givings-out were of an infinite distance
From his true meant design. Upon his place,
And with full line of his authority,
Governs Lord Angelo, a man whose blood

58 *snow-broth*: melted snow.

59 *wanton*: wilful.
motions: urges.

60 *rebate*: dull; the stress is on the second syllable.

62 *use and liberty*: the freedom that we have got used to.

70 *my pith of business*: the essence of my errand.

72 *censur'd*: condemned.

83 *would owe*: would wish to have them.

Is very snow-broth; one who never feels
The wanton stings and motions of the sense,
But doth rebate and blunt his natural edge
With profits of the mind: study and fast.
He, to give fear to use and liberty,
Which have for long run by the hideous law
As mice by lions, hath pick'd out an Act
Under whose heavy sense your brother's life
Falls into forfeit. He arrests him on it,
And follows close the rigour of the statute
To make him an example. All hope is gone,
Unless you have the grace by your fair prayer
To soften Angelo. And that's my pith of business
'Twixt you and your poor brother.

Isabella

Doth he so
Seek his life?

Lucio

Has censur'd him already,
And, as I hear, the provost hath a warrant
For's execution.

Isabella

Alas! What poor
Ability's in me to do him good?

Lucio

Assay the power you have.

Isabella

My power? Alas, I doubt.

Lucio

Our doubts are traitors
And makes us lose the good we oft might win,
By fearing to attempt. Go to Lord Angelo
And let him learn to know, when maidens sue
Men give like gods, but when they weep and kneel
All their petitions are as freely theirs
As they themselves would owe them.

Isabella

I'll see what I can do.

Lucio

But speedily.

86 *Mother*: Prioress.

Isabella

I will about it straight;
No longer staying but to give the Mother
Notice of my affair. I humbly thank you.
Commend me to my brother: soon at night
I'll send him certain word of my success.

Lucio

I take my leave of you.

Isabella

Good sir, adieu. [*Exeunt*

'Alas! What poor Ability's in me to do him good?' (*1*, 4, 74–5). Stella Gonet as Isabella, Royal Shakespeare Company, 1994.

'Prove it before these varlets here, thou honourable man, prove it!' (*2*, 1, 81–2) Norman Beaton as Angelo, Leslie Sands as Escalus, and Oscar James as Pompey, National Theatre, 1981.

ACT 2

Act 2 Scene 1
Angelo and Escalus hold their first trial: Froth is sent away with a warning, but Pompey is given a caution.

Scene 1

The Court Room: enter Angelo, Escalus, *and* Servants, *and a* Justice

Angelo
We must not make a scarecrow of the law,
Setting it up to fear the birds of prey,
And let it keep one shape till custom make it
Their perch and not their terror.

Escalus
Ay, but yet
Let us be keen, and rather cut a little
Than fall and bruise to death. Alas, this gentleman
Whom I would save had a most noble father.
Let but your honour know,
Whom I believe to be most strait in virtue,
That in the working of your own affections,
Had time coher'd with place, or place with wishing,
Or that the resolute acting of your blood
Could have attain'd th'effect of your own purpose,
Whether you had not sometime in your life
Err'd in this point which now you censure him,
And pull'd the law upon you.

Angelo
'Tis one thing to be tempted, Escalus,
Another thing to fall. I not deny
The jury passing on the prisoner's life
May in the sworn twelve have a thief or two
Guiltier than him they try: what's open made to
justice,
That justice seizes. What knows the laws
That thieves do pass on thieves? 'Tis very pregnant,
The jewel that we find, we stoop and take't,
Because we see it; but what we do not see
We tread upon and never think of it.

3 *custom*: familiarity.

5 *keen*: sharp, acute.

6 *fall*: drop, cause to fall.

9 *strait*: strict, rigorous.
virtue: morality, good living.

10 *affections*: desires.

11 *Had . . . place*: if time and place had been right.

12 *blood*: passions.

13 *effect*: achievement.

19 *passing*: passing judgement.

22–3 *What . . . thieves*: what do we know about laws that thieves pass on other thieves.

23 *pregnant*: obvious.

You may not so extenuate his offence
For I have had such faults; but rather tell me,
When I that censure him do so offend,
Let mine own judgement pattern out my death
And nothing come in partial. Sir, he must die.

Enter Provost

Escalus
Be it as your wisdom will.

Angelo
Where is the provost?

Provost
Here, if it like your honour.

Angelo
See that Claudio
Be executed by nine tomorrow morning.
Bring him his confessor, let him be prepar'd,
For that's the utmost of his pilgrimage. [*Exit* Provost

Escalus
Well, heaven forgive him, and forgive us all.
Some rise by sin and some by virtue fall,
Some run from breaks of ice and answer none,
And some condemned for a fault alone.

Enter Elbow *and* Officers *with* Froth *and* Pompey

Elbow
Come, bring them away. If these be good people in a commonweal, that do nothing but use their abuses in common houses, I know no law. Bring them away.

Angelo
How now, sir, what's your name, and what's the matter?

Elbow
If it please your honour, I am the poor duke's constable, and my name is Elbow. I do lean upon justice, sir, and do bring in here, before your good honour, two notorious benefactors.

Angelo
Benefactors? Well, what benefactors are they? Are they not malefactors?

28 *For*: because.

30 *mine own judgement*: the sentence that I pass (i.e. on Claudio).

31 *come in partial*: be admitted in extenuation.

36 *utmost . . . pilgrimage*: limit of his passage through life.

39–40 *Some . . . alone*: i.e. 'some break the ice many times and get away with it, others are caught with the first mistake'.

40 *condemned*: condemnèd.

42 *use their abuses*: carry on with their wicked ways.

43 *common houses*: brothels.

45–6 *the poor duke's constable*: i.e. the duke's poor constable.

46 *lean upon*: uphold; Elbow's verbal confusions ('malapropisms') resemble those of Shakespeare's earlier constable, Dogberry, in *Much Ado About Nothing*.

Elbow

If it please your honour, I know not well what they are: but precise villains they are, that I am sure of, and void of all profanation in the world that good Christians ought to have.

Escalus

This comes off well: here's a wise officer.

Angelo

Go to. What quality are they of? Elbow is your name? Why dost thou not speak, Elbow?

Pompey

He cannot, sir: he's out at elbow.

Angelo

What are you, sir?

Elbow

He, sir? A tapster, sir, parcel bawd, one that serves a bad woman, whose house, sir, was, as they say, plucked down in the suburbs; and now she professes a hot-house; which I think is a very ill house too.

Escalus

How know you that?

Elbow

My wife, sir, whom I detest before heaven and your honour—

Escalus

How? Thy wife?

Elbow

Ay, sir: whom I thank heaven is an honest woman—

Escalus

Dost thou detest her therefore?

Elbow

I say, sir, I will detest myself also, as well as she, that this house, if it be not a bawd's house, it is pity of her life, for it is a naughty house.

Escalus

How dost thou know that, constable?

Elbow

Marry, sir, by my wife, who, if she had been a woman cardinally given, might have been accused in fornication, adultery, and all uncleanliness there.

52 *precise*: puritanical.

53 *profanation*: Elbow perhaps intends 'profession' (= belief in God).

55 *comes off well*: is well spoken.

58 *out at elbow*: a) at a loss for words; b) shabby in dress.

60 *parcel*: part-time.

62–3 *professes . . . house*: pretends to keep a bath-house.

65 *detest*: Elbow means 'attest' or 'protest'.

71 *pity of her life*: a very sad thing for her.

72 *naughty*: wicked (the word had a stronger meaning in Shakespeare's day).

75 *cardinally*: i.e. 'carnally', lustfully.

Escalus

By the woman's means?

Elbow

Ay, sir, by Mistress Overdone's means. But as she spit in his face, so she defied him.

Pompey

Sir, if it please your honour, this is not so.

Elbow

Prove it before these varlets here, thou honourable man, prove it!

Escalus

Do you hear how he misplaces?

Pompey

Sir, she came in great with child; and longing, saving your honours' reverence, for stewed prunes. Sir, we had but two in the house, which at that very distant time stood, as it were, in a fruit dish, a dish of some three pence; your honours have seen such dishes, they are not china dishes, but very good dishes—

Escalus

Go to, go to: no matter for the dish, sir.

Pompey

No indeed, sir, not of a pin; you are therein in the right—but to the point: as I say, this Mistress Elbow, being, as I say, with child, and being great-bellied, and longing, as I said, for prunes, and having but two in the dish, as I said, Master Froth here, this very man, having eaten the rest, as I said, and, as I say, paying for them very honestly—for as you know, Master Froth, I could not give you three pence again—

Froth

No indeed.

Pompey

Very well. You being then, if you be remembered, cracking the stones of the foresaid prunes—

Froth

Ay, so I did indeed.

Pompey

Why, very well. I telling you then, if you be remembered, that such a one, and such a one, were past

79 *his*: i.e. Pompey's.

83 *misplaces*: i.e. 'varlets' and 'honourable'.

85 *stewed prunes*: The dish was popular in brothels ('the stews'); the Folio spelling 'prewyns' probably represents Pompey's pronunciation.

cure of the thing you wot of, unless they kept very good diet, as I told you—

Froth

All this is true.

Pompey

Why very well then—

Escalus

Come, you are a tedious fool, to the purpose: what was done to Elbow's wife, that he hath cause to complain of? Come me to what was done to her.

Pompey

Sir, your honour cannot come to that yet.

Escalus

No, sir, nor I mean it not.

Pompey

Sir, but you shall come to it, by your honour's leave; and I beseech you, look into Master Froth here, sir; a man of four score pound a year; whose father died at Hallowmas—was't not at Hallowmas, Master Froth?

Froth

All-Hallond Eve.

Pompey

Why, very well: I hope here be truths. He, sir, sitting, as I say, in a lower chair, sir—'twas in the Bunch of Grapes, where indeed you have a delight to sit, have you not?

Froth

I have so, because it is an open room, and good for winter.

Pompey

Why, very well then: I hope here be truths.

Angelo

This will last out a night in Russia
When nights are longest there. I'll take my leave,
And leave you to the hearing of the cause,
Hoping you'll find good cause to whip them all.
[*Exit*

Escalus

I think no less: good morrow to your lordship. Now, sir, come on: what was done to Elbow's wife, once more?

Pompey

Once, sir? There was nothing done to her once.

105 *the thing you wot of*: you-know-what—i.e. venereal disease.

111 *Come me*: get on, come to.

117 *Hallowmas*: All Saints' Day (1st November).

118 *All-Hallond Eve*: the evening before All Saints'.

120 *Bunch of Grapes*: Rooms in inns and hostels were designated by different names.

122 *open room*: public room (where a fire was kept in winter).

127 *cause*: case.

143 *supposed*: deposed, sworn.
a book: the Bible.

148–51 *respected*: Elbow means 'suspected', but Pompey (intending to confuse Elbow) uses the word in its correct sense.

Elbow
I beseech you, sir, ask him what this man did to my wife.

Pompey
I beseech your honour, ask me.

Escalus
Well, sir, what did this gentleman to her?

Pompey
I beseech you, sir, look in this gentleman's face. Good Master Froth, look upon his honour; 'tis for a good purpose. Doth your honour mark his face?

Escalus
Ay, sir, very well.

Pompey
Nay, I beseech you mark it well.

Escalus
Well, I do so.

Pompey
Doth your honour see any harm in his face?

Escalus
Why, no.

Pompey
I'll be supposed upon a book, his face is the worst thing about him: good then: if his face be the worst thing about him, how could Master Froth do the constable's wife any harm? I would know that of your honour.

Escalus
He's in the right, constable, what say you to it?

Elbow
First, and it like you, the house is a respected house; next, this is a respected fellow; and his mistress is a respected woman.

Pompey
By this hand, sir, his wife is a more respected person than any of us all.

Elbow
Varlet, thou liest! Thou liest, wicked varlet! The time is yet to come that she was ever respected with man, woman, or child.

Pompey
Sir, she was respected with him before he married with her.

158 *Justice or Iniquity*: These were stock characters in the Morality Plays of the fifteenth and sixteenth centuries.

159 *caitiff*: wretch.

160 *Hannibal*: Elbow seems to confuse Pompey with the Carthaginian general.

174 *to continue*: Elbow assumes that this is some kind of punishment.

Escalus

Which is the wiser here, Justice or Iniquity? Is this true?

Elbow

Oh, thou caitiff! Oh, thou varlet! Oh, thou wicked Hannibal! I respected with her, before I was married to her? If ever I was respected with her, or she with me, let not your worship think me the poor duke's officer! Prove this, thou wicked Hannibal, or I'll have mine action of battery on thee.

Escalus

If he took you a box o'th'ear, you might have your action of slander too.

Elbow

Marry, I thank your good worship for it. What is't your worship's pleasure I shall do with this wicked caitiff?

Escalus

Truly, officer, because he hath some offences in him that thou wouldst discover, if thou couldst, let him continue in his courses till thou knowst what they are.

Elbow

Marry, I thank your worship for it. Thou seest, thou wicked varlet, now, what's come upon thee. Thou art to continue, now, thou varlet, thou art to continue.

Escalus

Where were you born, friend?

Froth

Here in Vienna, sir.

Escalus

Are you of four score pounds a year?

Froth

Yes, and't please you, sir.

Escalus

So. [*To* Pompey] What trade are you of, sir?

Pompey

A tapster, a poor widow's tapster.

Escalus

Your mistress' name?

Pompey

Mistress Overdone.

187 *draw you*: a) draw ale for you; b) drain away your money; c) trick you; d) disembowel you.
hang them: give evidence that will cause them to hang.

190 *drawn in*: a) enticed in; b) cheated.

198 *Pompey the Great*: This was one of the three rulers of Rome in the first century BC.

200 *colour*: camouflage.

202 *would live*: has to make a living.

Escalus
Hath she had any more than one husband?

Pompey
Nine, sir: Overdone by the last.

Escalus
Nine? Come hither to me, Master Froth. Master Froth, I would not have you acquainted with tapsters; they will draw you, Master Froth, and you will hang them. Get you gone, and let me hear no more of you.

Froth
I thank your worship. For mine own part, I never come into any room in a taphouse, but I am drawn in.

Escalus
Well, no more of it, Master Froth. Farewell.

[*Exit* Froth

Come you hither to me, Master Tapster. What's your name, Master Tapster?

Pompey
Pompey.

Escalus
What else?

Pompey
Bum, sir.

Escalus
Troth, and your bum is the greatest thing about you, so that in the beastliest sense you are Pompey the Great. Pompey, you are partly a bawd, Pompey, howsoever you colour it in being a tapster, are you not? Come, tell me true, it shall be the better for you.

Pompey
Truly, sir, I am a poor fellow that would live.

Escalus
How would you live, Pompey? By being a bawd? What do you think of the trade, Pompey? Is it a lawful trade?

Pompey
If the law would allow it, sir.

Escalus
But the law will not allow it, Pompey; nor it shall not be allowed in Vienna.

208 *splay*: spay (= sterilize a female animal).
211 *will to't*: go and do it (i.e. commit fornication).
212 *drabs*: whores.
215 *heading*: beheading.
217 *commission*: authorization.
219 *three pence a bay*: i.e. dirt cheap; a 'bay' was defined as 'the space lying under one gable'.

224–5 *beat you . . . Caesar*: Pompey the Great was defeated by Julius Caesar at the battle of Pharsalia in 48 BC.
225 *shrewd*: severe.
231 *carman*: carter, carrier.
jade: nag, worthless horse.

237 *readiness*: proficiency.

Pompey

Does your worship mean to geld and splay all the youth of the city?

Escalus

No, Pompey.

Pompey

Truly, sir, in my poor opinion they will to't then. If your worship will take order for the drabs and the knaves, you need not to fear the bawds.

Escalus

There is pretty orders beginning, I can tell you: it is but heading and hanging.

Pompey

If you head and hang all that offend that way but for ten year together, you'll be glad to give out a commission for more heads. If this law hold in Vienna ten year, I'll rent the fairest house in it after three pence a bay. If you live to see this come to pass, say Pompey told you so.

Escalus

Thank you, good Pompey; and in requital of your prophecy, hark you: I advise you, let me not find you before me again upon any complaint whatsoever; no, not for dwelling where you do. If I do, Pompey, I shall beat you to your tent, and prove a shrewd Caesar to you: in plain dealing, Pompey, I shall have you whipped. So for this time, Pompey, fare you well.

Pompey

I thank your worship for your good counsel; [*Aside*] but I shall follow it as the flesh and fortune shall better determine.
Whip me? No, no, let carman whip his jade,
The valiant heart's not whipp'd out of his trade. [*Exit*

Escalus

Come hither to me, Master Elbow, come hither, Master Constable. How long have you been in this place of constable?

Elbow

Seven year, and a half, sir.

Escalus

I thought, by the readiness in the office, you had continued in it some time. You say seven years together?

Elbow

And a half, sir.

Escalus

Alas, it hath been great pains to you: they do you wrong to put you so oft upon't. Are there not men in your ward sufficient to serve it?

Elbow

Faith, sir, few of any wit in such matters. As they are chosen, they are glad to choose me for them; I do it for some piece of money, and go through with all.

Escalus

Look you bring me in the names of some six or seven, the most sufficient of your parish.

Elbow

To your worship's house, sir?

Escalus

To my house. Fare you well. [*Exit* Elbow

What's a clock, think you?

Justice

Eleven, sir.

Escalus

I pray you home to dinner with me.

Justice

I humbly thank you.

Escalus

It grieves me for the death of Claudio,
But there's no remedy.

Justice

Lord Angelo is severe.

Escalus

It is but needful.
Mercy is not itself that oft looks so,
Pardon is still the nurse of second woe.
But yet, poor Claudio; there is no remedy. Come, sir.

[*Exeunt*

241 *put you . . . upon't*: make you do the job so often.
ward: administrative district.

242 *sufficient*: competent enough.

243–5 *As . . . money*: The office, shared between community householders, was unpaid—and those unwilling to carry out the duties could pay for a substitute.

245 *go through with all*: get on with it.

259 *Pardon . . . woe*: forgiveness of one crime always leads to another.

Act 2 Scene 2
Isabella pleads with Angelo for her brother's life—but her words have an unexpected effect.

SCENE 2

Angelo's office: enter Provost and a Servant

Servant
He's hearing of a cause, he will come straight,
I'll tell him of you.
Provost
Pray you do. [*Exit* Servant
I'll know
His pleasure, may be he will relent. Alas,
He hath but as offended in a dream.
All sects, all ages smack of this vice, and he
To die for't?

Enter Angelo

Angelo
Now what's the matter, provost?
Provost
Is it your will Claudio shall die tomorrow?
Angelo
Did not I tell thee yea? Hadst thou not order?
Why dost thou ask again?
Provost
Lest I might be too rash:
Under your good correction, I have seen
When, after execution, judgement hath
Repented o'er his doom.
Angelo
Go to; let that be mine.
Do you your office, or give up your place,
And you shall well be spar'd.
Provost
I crave your honour's pardon:
What shall be done, sir, with the groaning Juliet?
She's very near her hour.
Angelo
Dispose of her
To some more fitter place, and that with speed.

4 *but as . . . dream*: offended but without being conscious of what he was doing.
5 *sects*: classes.
smack of: indulge in.
10 *Under*: subject to.
11 *judgement*: the judge.
12 *doom*: sentence.
mine: my business.
14 *you . . . spar'd*: we can manage well enough without you.
16 *groaning*: in labour.
17 *hour*: time of giving birth.

Enter Servant

Servant
Here is the sister of the man condemn'd,
Desires access to you.

Angelo
Hath he a sister?

Provost
Ay, my good lord, a very virtuous maid,
And to be shortly of a sisterhood,
If not already.

Angelo
Well. Let her be admitted. [*Exit* Servant
See you the fornicatress be remov'd.
Let her have needful, but not lavish, means.
There shall be order for't.

Enter Lucio *and* Isabella

Provost
Save your honour. [*Going*]

Angelo
Stay a little while. [*To* Isabella] Y'are welcome: what's your will?

Isabella
I am a woeful suitor to your honour,
Please but your honour hear me.

Angelo
Well; what's your suit?

Isabella
There is a vice that most I do abhor,
And most desire should meet the blow of justice;
For which I would not plead, but that I must,
For which I must not plead, but that I am
At war 'twixt will and will not.

Angelo
Well; the matter?

Isabella
I have a brother is condemn'd to die.
I do beseech you, let it be his fault,
And not my brother.

22 *sisterhood*: order of nuns.

26 *Save*: God save.

36 *let . . . fault*: Let it be the fault that is condemned.

40 *the very . . . function*: only the appearance of a function.

41 *fine the faults*: penalize the faults. *whose fine*: the punishment for which. *record*: law, the statute books.

53 *Look what . . . do*: Angelo's words seem to emphasize the arbitrariness of his judgement—an arbitrariness that Claudio apparently accepted (*1*, 2, 110–11).

Provost
[*Aside*] Heaven give thee moving graces!

Angelo
Condemn the fault, and not the actor of it?
Why, every fault's condemn'd ere it be done.
Mine were the very cipher of a function
To fine the faults, whose fine stands in record,
And let go by the actor.

Isabella
Oh just but severe law:
I had a brother then. Heaven keep your honour.
[*Going*]

Lucio
[*To* Isabella] Give't not o'er so: to him again, entreat him,
Kneel down before him, hang upon his gown.
You are too cold. If you should need a pin,
You could not with more tame a tongue desire it:
To him, I say.

Isabella
Must he needs die?

Angelo
Maiden, no remedy.

Isabella
Yes: I do think that you might pardon him,
And neither heaven nor man grieve at the mercy.

Angelo
I will not do't.

Isabella
But can you if you would?

Angelo
Look what I will not, that I cannot do.

Isabella
But might you do't, and do the world no wrong,
If so your heart were touch'd with that remorse
As mine is to him?

Angelo
He's sentenc'd, 'tis too late.

Lucio
[*To* Isabella] You are too cold.

Isabella

Too late? Why, no; I that do speak a word
May call it again. Well, believe this:
No ceremony that to great ones longs,
Not the king's crown, nor the deputed sword,
The marshal's truncheon, nor the judge's robe
Become them with one half so good a grace
As mercy does.
If he had been as you, and you as he,
You would have slipp'd like him, but he like you
Would not have been so stern.

Angelo

Pray you be gone.

Isabella

I would to heaven I had your potency,
And you were Isabel: should it then be thus?
No. I would tell what 'twere to be a judge,
And what a prisoner.

Lucio

[*Aside*] Ay, touch him, there's the vein.

Angelo

Your brother is a forfeit of the law,
And you but waste your words.

Isabella

Alas, alas!
Why all the souls that were, were forfeit once,
And he that might the vantage best have took
Found out the remedy. How would you be
If he, which is the top of judgement, should
But judge you as you are? Oh, think on that,
And mercy then will breathe within your lips
Like man new made.

Angelo

Be you content, fair maid,
It is the law, not I, condemn your brother.
Were he my kinsman, brother, or my son,
It should be thus with him: he must die tomorrow.

Isabella

Tomorrow? Oh, that's sudden! Spare him, spare him!
He's not prepar'd for death. Even for our kitchens
We kill the fowl of season: shall we serve heaven

60 *ceremony*: accessory, symbolic attribute.
longs: pertains to.

61 *deputed sword*: sword symbolizing divine justice deputed to earthly rulers.

62 *marshal's truncheon*: fieldmarshal's baton.

68 *potency*: executive power; Isabella's language in this scene is heavy with (unconscious) sexual overtones.

73 *Your brother*: your brother's life.

75–7 *all the souls . . . remedy*: The central doctrine of the Christian faith: 'All have sinned, and come short of the glory of God', but all can be saved 'through the redemption that is in Jesus Christ' (Romans 3: 23–4).

76 *he*: God.
vantage: advantage, opportunity (to punish mankind).

80–1 *mercy . . . made*: the mercy of God will breathe through your lips as though you were a new man; many places in the Bible (New Testament) speak of the Christian as being re-born—'Therefore if any man be in Christ, he is a new creature' (2 Corinthians 5:17).

With less respect than we do minister
To our gross selves? Good, good my lord, bethink you.
Who is it that hath died for this offence?
There's many have committed it.

Lucio

[*Aside*] Ay, well said.

Angelo

The law hath not been dead, though it hath slept.
Those many had not dar'd to do that evil
If the first that did th'edict infringe
Had answer'd for his deed. Now 'tis awake,
Takes note of what is done, and like a prophet
Looks in a glass that shows what future evils—
Either now, or by remissness new conceiv'd,
And so in progress to be hatch'd and born—
Are now to have no successive degrees,
But here they live to end.

Isabella

Yet show some pity.

Angelo

I show it most of all when I show justice;
For then I pity those I do not know,
Which a dismiss'd offence would after gall,
And do him right, that answering one foul wrong
Lives not to act another. Be satisfied.
Your brother dies tomorrow. Be content.

Isabella

So you must be the first that gives this sentence,
And he, that suffers. Oh, it is excellent
To have a giant's strength, but it is tyrannous
To use it like a giant.

Lucio

[*Aside*] That's well said.

Isabella

Could great men thunder
As Jove himself does, Jove would ne'er be quiet,
For every pelting, petty officer
Would use his heaven for thunder—
Nothing but thunder. Merciful heaven,
Thou rather with thy sharp and sulphurous bolt
Splits the unwedgeable and gnarled oak

96 *answer'd for*: paid the penalty of.

98 *glass . . . future*: i.e. a 'perspective glass', cut so as to reproduce the reflected image.

99 *remissness*: neglect.

101 *to have . . . degrees*: are to go no further.

105 *dismiss'd*: forgiven.
would . . . gall: would give trouble later on.

106 *do him right*: let him [i.e. the criminal] have justice.

115 *Jove*: The king of the classical gods (often pictured with a thunderbolt in his hand).

116 *pelting*: paltry, insignificant.

119 *sulphurous bolt*: It was thought that the brimstone ('sulphurous') thunderbolt was always accompanied by the destructive lightning.

120 *gnarled*: gnarlèd.

Than the soft myrtle; but man, proud man,
Dress'd in a little brief authority,
Most ignorant of what he's most assur'd,
His glassy essence, like an angry ape
Plays such fantastic tricks before high heaven
As makes the angels weep; who, with our spleens,
Would all themselves laugh mortal.

Lucio

[*Aside*] Oh, to him, to him, wench, he will relent.
He's coming: I perceive't.

Provost

[*Aside*] Pray heaven she win him!

Isabella

We cannot weigh our brother with ourself.
Great men may jest with saints: 'tis wit in them,
But in the less foul profanation.

Lucio

[*Aside*] Thou'rt i'th'right, girl, more o'that!

Isabella

That in the captain's but a choleric word
Which in the soldier is flat blasphemy.

Lucio

[*Aside*] Art avis'd o'that? More on't.

Angelo

Why do you put these sayings upon me?

Isabella

Because authority, though it err like others,
Hath yet a kind of medicine in itself
That skins the vice o'th'top. Go to your bosom,
Knock there, and ask your heart what it doth know
That's like my brother's fault. If it confess
A natural guiltiness, such as is his,
Let it not sound a thought upon your tongue
Against my brother's life.

Angelo

[*Aside*] She speaks, and 'tis such sense
That my sense breeds with it. [*To* Isabella] Fare you well.

Isabella

Gentle my lord, turn back.

124 *his glassy essence*: his own frail human nature.

126–7 *with our spleens . . . mortal*: if they were made like us, would laugh themselves to death; the spleen was believed to be the source of laughter (and melancholy).

130 *We . . . ourself*: Isabella may be speaking generally ('we can't judge others by our own standards') or personally, referring directly to Claudio.

131 *jest with*: make jokes about, speak lightly of.

134–5 *That . . . blasphemy*: a curse from an officer is only an expression of annoyance, but from a common soldier it is downright ('flat') blasphemy.

136 *Art . . . that*: have you discovered that.

137 *Why . . . me*: why are you telling this to me.

140 *skins . . . top*: grows a new skin to cover up the weakness.

144 *sound*: utter.

146 *such sense*: such meaning.

147 *my sense*: my sensual desire.
breeds with: is stimulated by.

154 *fond sickles*: silly little coins (Hebrew 'shekels').
tested: pure (see *1*, 1, 35–6 note).
155 *stones*: precious stones.
156 *fancy*: tastes, fashion.
158 *preserved souls*: preservèd; Isabella's sister nuns, protected from evil by their renunciation of the world.
164 *cross*: are at cross-purposes; Angelo's desire for Isabella is contrary to her wish for his safety.

Angelo
I will bethink me. Come again tomorrow.

Isabella
Hark how I'll bribe you—good my lord, turn back.

Angelo
How? Bribe me?

Isabella
Ay, with such gifts that heaven shall share with you.

Lucio
[*Aside*] You had marr'd all else.

Isabella
Not with fond sickles of the tested gold,
Or stones whose rate are either rich or poor
As fancy values them; but with true prayers,
That shall be up at heaven and enter there
Ere sun rise—prayers from preserved souls,
From fasting maids whose minds are dedicate
To nothing temporal.

Angelo
Well; come to me tomorrow.

Lucio
[*To* Isabella] Go to. 'Tis well. Away.

Isabella
Heaven keep your honour safe.

Angelo
[*Aside*] Amen.
For I am that way going to temptation
Where prayers cross.

Isabella
At what hour tomorrow
Shall I attend your lordship?

Angelo
At any time 'fore noon.

Isabella
Save your honour.
[*Exeunt* Isabella, Lucio, *and* Provost

Angelo
From thee: even from thy virtue.
What's this? What's this? Is this her fault, or mine?
The tempter or the tempted, who sins most, ha?
Not she: nor doth she tempt: but it is I

171 *carrion*: dead carcass.
172 *Corrupt . . . season*: rot in the life-giving sunshine.
173 *betray our sense*: arouse our sexual desires.
174 *lightness*: licentiousness.
175 *raze*: pull down, destroy.
176 *pitch*: establish.
184 *enemy*: the devil.
188 *double*: deceptive, double-dealing.
190 *Ever*: always.
191 *fond*: infatuated.

That, lying by the violet in the sun,
Do as the carrion does, not as the flower,
Corrupt with virtuous season. Can it be
That modesty may more betray our sense
Than women's lightness? Having waste ground enough
Shall we desire to raze the sanctuary
And pitch our evils there? Oh fie, fie, fie,
What dost thou or what art thou, Angelo?
Dost thou desire her foully for those things
That make her good? Oh, let her brother live:
Thieves for their robbery have authority
When judges steal themselves. What, do I love her
That I desire to hear her speak again
And feast upon her eyes? What is't I dream on?
Oh cunning enemy that, to catch a saint,
With saints dost bait thy hook! Most dangerous
Is that temptation that doth goad us on
To sin in loving virtue. Never could the strumpet
With all her double vigour, art and nature,
Once stir my temper; but this virtuous maid
Subdues me quite. Ever till now
When men were fond, I smil'd, and wondered how.
[*Exit*

Act 2 Scene 3
The duke visits the prison and talks with Juliet.

3 *Bound . . . order*: bound by my holy order to perform works of charity. *blessed*: blessèd.

11 *flaws*: follies, weaknesses.

12 *blister'd her report*: sullied her reputation.

21 *arraign*: examine.
22 *sound*: genuine.
23 *hollowly put on*: falsely assumed, merely pretended.

SCENE 3

The prison: enter Duke [*disguised as a friar*] *and* Provost

Duke
Hail to you, provost—so I think you are.
Provost
I am the provost. What's your will, good friar?
Duke
Bound by my charity and my blessed order
I come to visit the afflicted spirits
Here in the prison. Do me the common right
To let me see them and to make me know
The nature of their crimes, that I may minister
To them accordingly.
Provost
I would do more than that, if more were needful.

Enter Juliet

Look, here comes one, a gentlewoman of mine,
Who, falling in the flaws of her own youth,
Hath blister'd her report. She is with child
And he that got it, sentenc'd—a young man
More fit to do another such offence
Than die for this.
Duke
When must he die?
Provost
As I do think, tomorrow.
[*To* Juliet] I have provided for you, stay awhile
And you shall be conducted.
Duke
Repent you, fair one, of the sin you carry?
Juliet
I do, and bear the shame most patiently.
Duke
I'll teach you how you shall arraign your conscience
And try your penitence if it be sound
Or hollowly put on.

28 *heavier*: more serious, harder to bear (because she must bear the child).

31 *As that*: only because.

33 *as*: because.

38 *instruction*: spiritual advice.

39 *Benedicite*: God bless you.

40–2 *injurious . . . horror*: Juliet's love is 'injurious' (= cruel) because although her pregnancy saves her from death, it will always remind her of the horror of Claudio's death.

Juliet
I'll gladly learn.

Duke
Love you the man that wrong'd you?

Juliet
Yes, as I love the woman that wrong'd him.

Duke
So then it seems your most offenceful act
Was mutually committed.

Juliet
Mutually.

Duke
Then was your sin of heavier kind than his.

Juliet
I do confess it, and repent it, father.

Duke
'Tis meet so, daughter, but lest you do repent
As that the sin hath brought you to this shame—
Which sorrow is always toward ourselves not heaven,
Showing we would not spare heaven as we love it,
But as we stand in fear—

Juliet
I do repent me as it is an evil
And take the shame with joy.

Duke
There rest.
Your partner, as I hear, must die tomorrow,
And I am going with instruction to him.
Grace go with you, *Benedicite*. [*Exit*

Juliet
Must die tomorrow? Oh, injurious love
That respites me a life whose very comfort
Is still a dying horror!

Provost
'Tis pity of him. [*Exeunt*

Act 2 Scene 4
Angelo confronts his own predicament before renewing his offer and threat to Isabella.

2 *several*: separate, different.

3 *invention*: imagination.

4 *Heaven*: God; the line has perhaps been censored (see 'Source, Date, and Text', p.xxvii).

5 *chew*: mumble.

7 *my conception*: the idea I have formed.
state: statecraft.

9 *sere*: dry, faded.
gravity: dignified solemnity.

11 *boot*: advantage.
idle plume: feathered cap of a frivolous courtier.

12 *for vain*: in useless vanity.
place . . . form: high position and formal manner.

13 *case*: outward appearance.

15 *Blood . . . blood*: Angelo recognizes that despite all outward appearances, human nature with its sexual desires cannot be anything other than it is.

16–17 *Let's write . . . crest*: even if we write 'Good Angel' on his horn, the devil will not change his nature.

20 *muster*: rush.

27 *general . . . king*: all the subjects of a popular monarch (see 'Source, Date, and Text', p.xxvii)

28 *Quit . . . part*: leave what they ought to be doing.
obsequious fondness: foolish flattery.

29 *untaught*: uncouth.

Scene 4

Angelo*'s office: enter* Angelo

Angelo
When I would pray and think, I think and pray
To several subjects: heaven hath my empty words
Whilst my invention, hearing not my tongue,
Anchors on Isabel. Heaven in my mouth
As if I did not only chew his name,
And in my heart the strong and swelling evil
Of my conception. The state whereon I studied
Is like a good thing being often read
Grown sere and tedious. Yea, my gravity,
Wherein—let no man hear me—I take pride,
Could I with boot change for an idle plume
Which the air beats for vain. Oh place, oh form,
How often dost thou with thy case, thy habit,
Wrench awe from fools and tie the wiser souls
To thy false seeming. Blood, thou art blood:
Let's write 'Good Angel' on the devil's horn,
'Tis not the devil's crest. How now, who's there?

Enter Servant

Servant
One Isabel, a sister, desires access to you.

Angelo
Teach her the way. [*Exit* Servant
Oh, heavens,
Why does my blood thus muster to my heart,
Making both it unable for itself
And dispossessing all my other parts
Of necessary fitness?
So play the foolish throngs with one that swoons,
Come all to help him and so stop the air
By which he should revive; and even so
The general subject to a well-wish'd king
Quit their own part and in obsequious fondness
Crowd to his presence, where their untaught love
Must needs appear offence.

Enter Isabella

How now, fair maid?

Isabella

I am come to know your pleasure.

Angelo

That you might know it would much better please me
Than to demand what 'tis. Your brother cannot live.

Isabella

Even so. Heaven keep your honour.

Angelo

Yet may he live a while—and it may be
As long as you or I—yet he must die.

Isabella

Under your sentence?

Angelo

Yea.

Isabella

When, I beseech you? That, in his reprieve,
Longer or shorter, he may be so fitted
That his soul sicken not.

Angelo

Ha! Fie, these filthy vices! It were as good
To pardon him that hath from nature stolen
A man already made, as to remit
Their saucy sweetness, that do coin heaven's image
In stamps that are forbid. 'Tis all as easy
Falsely to take away a life true made
As to put metal in restrained means
To make a false one.

Isabella

'Tis set down so in heaven, but not in earth.

Angelo

Say you so? Then I shall pose you quickly.
Which had you rather: that the most just law
Now took your brother's life, or to redeem him
Give up your body to such sweet uncleanness
As she that he hath stain'd?

Isabella

Sir, believe this:
I had rather give my body than my soul.

31 *your pleasure*: what it is you want.

32 *know it*: understand what it is without being told.

39 *fitted*: spiritually prepared.

42–3 *him . . . made*: some man who has taken the life of another.

43 *remit*: pardon.

44–5 *coin . . . forbid*: beget an illegitimate child (which, like all human beings, is made in the 'image' of God).

47 *restrained*: restrainèd; forbidden.

50 *pose*: put a difficult question to.

Angelo
I talk not of your soul. Our compell'd sins
Stand more for number than for accompt.

Isabella
How say you?

Angelo
Nay, I'll not warrant that, for I can speak
Against the thing I say. Answer to this:
I, now the voice of the recorded law,
Pronounce a sentence on your brother's life.
Might there not be a charity in sin
To save this brother's life?

Isabella
Please you to do't,
I'll take it as a peril to my soul,
It is no sin at all but charity.

Angelo
Pleas'd you to do't, at peril of your soul,
Were equal poise of sin and charity.

Isabella
That I do beg his life, if it be sin,
Heaven let me bear it. You granting of my suit,
If that be sin, I'll make it my morn-prayer
To have it added to the faults of mine
And nothing of your answer.

Angelo
Nay, but hear me,
Your sense pursues not mine: either you are ignorant
Or seem so crafty, and that's not good.

Isabella
Let me be ignorant and in nothing good
But graciously to know I am no better.

Angelo
Thus wisdom wishes to appear most bright
When it doth tax itself, as these black masks
Proclaim an enshield beauty ten times louder
Than beauty could, display'd. But mark me.
To be received plain, I'll speak more gross:
Your brother is to die.

Isabella
So.

56–7 *Our compell'd sins . . . accompt*: sins that we are forced to commit are recorded but we do not have to account for them.
58 *How say you*: do you mean that.
59 *warrant*: guarantee.
59–60 *I can . . . say*: I can argue on both sides of a question; Angelo will employ his legal training in an attempt to trick Isabella.
63 *a charity in sin*: a charitable sin (or a sinful charity).
64 *Please . . . do't*: if you would agree to do this (Isabella is assuming that Angelo refers to the possible sin of pardoning a guilty man).
67 *Pleas'd . . . do't*: if you would be willing to do this (i.e. satisfy Angelo's desires).
68 *equal poise*: equal balance.
73 *of your answer*: that you have to answer for.
75 *seem so crafty*: seem ignorant in your craftiness.
77 *graciously . . . better*: have the humility to know that I am nothing better.
79 *tax*: accuse.
these black masks: the black masks that women wear.
80 *enshield*: protected (as with a shield), defended.
82 *received*: receivèd; understood.

Angelo

And his offence is so as it appears
Accountant to the law upon that pain.

Isabella

True.

Angelo

Admit no other way to save his life—
As I subscribe not that, nor any other,
But in the loss of question—that you, his sister,
Finding yourself desir'd of such a person
Whose credit with the judge, or own great place,
Could fetch your brother from the manacles
Of the all-binding law, and that there were
No earthly mean to save him, but that either
You must lay down the treasures of your body
To this suppos'd, or else to let him suffer:
What would you do?

Isabella

As much for my poor brother as myself:
That is, were I under the terms of death,
Th'impression of keen whips I'd wear as rubies,
And strip myself to death as to a bed
That longing have been sick for, ere I'd yield
My body up to shame.

Angelo

Then must your brother die.

Isabella

And 'twere the cheaper way:
Better it were a brother died at once,
Than that a sister by redeeming him
Should die for ever.

Angelo

Were not you then as cruel as the sentence
That you have slander'd so?

Isabella

Ignomy in ransom and free pardon
Are of two houses: lawful mercy
Is nothing kin to foul redemption.

86 *Accountant . . . pain*: forfeit to the law on that penalty.

89 *I subscribe not*: I'm not saying there is.

90 *But . . . question*: except for the sake of argument.

94 *all-binding law*: law that binds all under the same restraints.

96 *treasures of your body*: your virginity.

107 *at once*: immediately, at a single stroke.

109 *die for ever*: suffer eternal damnation.

112 *Ignomy*: ignominy; the contracted form was in use until the early nineteenth century.

113 *of two houses*: from different families, not related.

Angelo
You seem'd of late to make the law a tyrant,
And rather prov'd the sliding of your brother
A merriment than a vice.

Isabella
Oh, pardon me, my lord, it oft falls out
To have what we would have, we speak not what we mean.
I something do excuse the thing I hate
For his advantage that I dearly love.

Angelo
We are all frail.

Isabella
Else let my brother die,
If not a fedary but only he
Owe and succeed thy weakness.

Angelo
Nay, women are frail too.

Isabella
Ay, as the glasses where they view themselves,
Which are as easy broke as they make forms.
Women? Help heaven, men their creation mar
In profiting by them. Nay, call us ten times frail,
For we are soft as our complexions are,
And credulous to false prints.

Angelo
I think it well,
And from this testimony of your own sex—
Since I suppose we are made to be no stronger
Than faults may shake our frames—let me be bold;
I do arrest your words. Be that you are,
That is, a woman; if you be more, you're none.
If you be one, as you are well express'd
By all external warrants, show it now
By putting on the destin'd livery.

Isabella
I have no tongue but one. Gentle my lord,
Let me entreat you speak the former language.

Angelo
Plainly conceive, I love you.

116 *sliding*: lapse, slipping (into sin).
117 *merriment*: nonsense, trviality.
122 *frail*: morally weak.
123 *fedary*: confederate, accomplice.
124 *Owe . . . weakness*: owns and inherits that same frailty.
127 *make forms*: show reflections, multiply images.
128–9 *men . . . by them*: men, created in the image of God, debase themselves in their relations with women.
131 *credulous to*: easily impressed by. *false prints*: counterfeits.
133–4 *no stronger . . . frames*: not so strong that we can't be shaken by temptation.
135 *arrest your words*: take you at your own words.
136 *a woman*: i.e. and therefore 'soft' and 'credulous to false prints'. *more*: more resistant than a woman should be. *none*: not a true woman.
137 *express'd*: shown to be.
139 *putting . . . livery*: entering into the service you were destined for. *livery*: distinctive uniform or badge of a servant.
142 *conceive*: understand.

Isabella
My brother did love Juliet
And you tell me that he shall die for't.

Angelo
He shall not, Isabel, if you give me love.

Isabella
I know your virtue hath a licence in't
Which seems a little fouler than it is
To pluck on others.

Angelo
Believe me on mine honour,
My words express my purpose.

Isabella
Ha! Little honour to be much believ'd,
And most pernicious purpose. Seeming, seeming.
I will proclaim thee, Angelo, look for't.
Sign me a present pardon for my brother,
Or with an outstretch'd throat I'll tell the world aloud
What man thou art.

Angelo
Who will believe thee, Isabel?
My unsoil'd name, th'austereness of my life,
My vouch against you, and my place i'th'state,
Will so your accusation overweigh
That you shall stifle in your own report
And smell of calumny. I have begun,
And now I give my sensual race the rein.
Fit thy consent to my sharp appetite,
Lay by all nicety and prolixious blushes
That banish what they sue for, redeem thy brother
By yielding up thy body to my will,
Or else he must not only die the death
But thy unkindness shall his death draw out
To lingering sufferance. Answer me tomorrow,
Or by th'affection that now guides me most
I'll prove a tyrant to him. As for you,
Say what you can, my false o'erweighs your true. [*Exit*

Isabella
To whom should I complain? Did I tell this
Who would believe me? Oh, perilous mouths
That bear in them one and the self-same tongue,

146–8 *I know . . . others*: I understand that your power allows you to make things seem worse than they are in order to bring out other faults.

152 *proclaim*: denounce.

153 *present*: immediate.

157 *vouch*: formal statement.

159 *stifle*: choke yourself.

160 *smell of calumny*: get a reputation for slander.

161 *give . . . rein*: let my passions go unchecked.

163 *nicety*: delicacy, modesty.
prolixious: time-wasting, superfluous (Shakespeare's own coinage from 'prolix').

168 *lingering sufferance*: long drawn-out torture.

169 *affection*: passion.

175 *approof*: approval.

179 *by prompture . . . blood*: under pressure from his physical urges.

181 *tender down*: pay down.

Either of condemnation or approof,
Bidding the law make curtsy to their will,
Hooking both right and wrong to th'appetite
To follow as it draws. I'll to my brother.
Though he hath fall'n by prompture of the blood
Yet hath he in him such a mind of honour
That had he twenty heads to tender down
On twenty bloody blocks he'd yield them up
Before his sister should her body stoop
To such abhorr'd pollution.
Then Isabel live chaste, and brother die:
More than our brother is our chastity.
I'll tell him yet of Angelo's request,
And fit his mind to death for his soul's rest. [*Exit*

'Death is a fearful thing.' (*3*, 1, 116) Josette Simon as Isabella and Hakeem Kae-Kazim as Claudio, Royal Shakespeare Company, 1987.

ACT 3

Act 3 Scene 1
Counselling Claudio, the 'friar' overhears Isabella when she tells her brother of Angelo's proposition, and makes plans to thwart the duke's deputy.

SCENE 1

The prison: Claudio*'s cell. Enter* Duke [*disguised as a friar*], Claudio, *and* Provost

Duke
So then you hope of pardon from Lord Angelo?
Claudio
The miserable have no other medicine
But only hope.
I have hope to live, and am prepar'd to die.
Duke
Be absolute for death: either death or life
Shall thereby be the sweeter. Reason thus with life:
If I do lose thee I do lose a thing
That none but fools would keep; a breath thou art,
Servile to all the skyey influences
That dost this habitation where thou keepst
Hourly afflict. Merely, thou art death's fool,
For him thou labour'st by thy flight to shun
And yet runn'st toward him still. Thou art not noble,
For all th'accommodations that thou bear'st
Are nurs'd by baseness; thou'rt by no means valiant,
For thou dost fear the soft and tender fork
Of a poor worm. Thy best of rest is sleep,
And that thou oft provok'st, yet grossly fear'st
Thy death, which is no more. Thou art not thyself,
For thou exists on many a thousand grains
That issue out of dust. Happy thou art not,
For what thou hast not still thou striv'st to get,
And what thou hast, forget'st. Thou art not certain,
For thy complexion shifts to strange effects
After the moon. If thou art rich thou'rt poor,
For like an ass whose back with ingots bows
Thou bear'st thy heavy riches but a journey
And death unloads thee. Friend hast thou none,

5 *absolute*: completely decided upon.

9 *skyey influences*: astrological influences.
10 *dost*: A singular verb for the plural subject 'influences'.
keepst: dwellest.
11 *Merely*: quite simply.
fool: plaything.
14 *accommodations*: clothing, trappings of civilized existence.
15 *nurs'd by baseness*: nourished out of the base matter of life.
16 *fork*: forked tongue.
17 *worm*: snake.
18 *provok'st*: try to induce.
19 *Thou . . . thyself*: you are not complete in yourself.
21 *issue . . . dust*: God told Adam that he would die, 'because thou art dust, and to dust shalt thou return' (Genesis 3:19).
22 *still*: always.
23 *certain*: constant.
24–5 *thy complexion . . . moon*: your constitution alters in strange ways under the influence of the moon.
26 *ingots*: bars of gold and silver.

For thine own bowels which do call thee sire,
The mere effusion of thy proper loins
Do curse the gout, serpigo, and the rheum
For ending thee no sooner. Thou hast nor youth nor age,
But as it were an after-dinner's sleep,
Dreaming on both: for all thy blessed youth
Becomes as aged and doth beg the alms
Of palsied eld; and when thou art old and rich,
Thou hast neither heat, affection, limb, nor beauty
To make thy riches pleasant. What's yet in this
That bears the name of life? Yet in this life
Lie hid moe thousand deaths; yet death we fear
That makes these odds all even.

Claudio

I humbly thank you.
To sue to live, I find I seek to die,
And seeking death, find life: let it come on.

Isabella

[*Within*] What ho, peace here; grace and good company.

Provost

Who's there? Come in, the wish deserves a welcome.

Duke

[*To* Claudio] Dear sir, ere long I'll visit you again.

Claudio

Most holy sir, I thank you.

Enter Isabella

Isabella

My business is a word or two with Claudio.

Provost

And very welcome. Look, signior, here's your sister.

Duke

Provost, a word with you.

Provost

As many as you please.

Duke

Bring me to hear them speak where I may be conceal'd.

---

29 *thine own bowels*: your children (a biblical expression).

30 *mere effusion . . . loins*: your very own offspring.

31 *serpigo*: skin disease spreading over the entire body, psoriasis.
rheum: catarrh.

33 *after-dinner's sleep*: afternoon nap; the main meal, dinner, was eaten around noon.

35 *aged*: agèd.

35–6 *Becomes . . . eld*: becomes like old age in its dependency on the charity of feeble older parents.

37 *heat . . . limb*: energy, passion, or strength of limb.

40 *moe thousand*: a thousand more.

42–3 *To sue . . . life*: Although the 'friar' has offered no such comfort, Claudio seems to be reminding himself of Christ's promise, 'He that findeth his life shall lose it, and he that loseth his life for my sake shall find it' (Matthew 10:39).

52s.d. *conceal themselves*: The audience—and readers—must never forget the hidden presence of the duke and provost.

58 *everlasting lieger*: permanent ambassador.

59 *appointment*: preparation.

66 *durance*: imprisonment.

68 *vastidity*: vastness, immensity.

69 *determin'd scope*: fixed limitation.

71 *Would . . . bear*: would deprive your life of honour as a tree trunk is stripped of bark.

74 *entertain*: take into consideration.

Duke *and* Provost *conceal themselves*

Claudio
Now, sister, what's the comfort?
Isabella
Why,
As all comforts are: most good, most good indeed.
Lord Angelo, having affairs to heaven,
Intends you for his swift ambassador,
Where you shall be an everlasting lieger;
Therefore your best appointment make with speed,
Tomorrow you set on.
Claudio
Is there no remedy?
Isabella
None, but such remedy as, to save a head,
To cleave a heart in twain.
Claudio
But is there any?
Isabella
Yes, brother, you may live;
There is a devilish mercy in the judge,
If you'll implore it, that will free your life,
But fetter you till death.
Claudio
Perpetual durance?
Isabella
Ay, just, perpetual durance, a restraint,
Though all the world's vastidity you had,
To a determin'd scope.
Claudio
But in what nature?
Isabella
In such a one as you, consenting to't,
Would bark your honour from that trunk you bear
And leave you naked.
Claudio
Let me know the point.
Isabella
Oh, I do fear thee, Claudio, and I quake
Lest thou a feverous life shouldst entertain

And six or seven winters more respect
Than a perpetual honour. Dar'st thou die?
The sense of death is most in apprehension,
And the poor beetle that we tread upon
In corporal sufferance finds a pang as great
As when a giant dies.

Claudio

Why give you me this shame?
Think you I can a resolution fetch
From flowery tenderness? If I must die
I will encounter darkness as a bride
And hug it in mine arms.

Isabella

There spake my brother, there my father's grave
Did utter forth a voice. Yes, thou must die:
Thou art too noble to conserve a life
In base appliances. This outward-sainted deputy
Whose settled visage and deliberate word
Nips youth i'th'head and follies doth enew
As falcon doth the fowl, is yet a devil:
His filth within being cast, he would appear
A pond as deep as hell.

Claudio

The prenzie Angelo?

Isabella

Oh 'tis the cunning livery of hell
The damned'st body to invest and cover
In prenzie guards. Dost thou think, Claudio,
If I would yield him my virginity
Thou might'st be freed!

Claudio

Oh, heavens, it cannot be!

Isabella

Yes, he would give't thee; from this rank offence
So to offend him still. This night's the time
That I should do what I abhor to name,
Or else thou diest tomorrow.

Claudio

Thou shalt not do't.

75 *respect*: value.

77 *apprehension*: imaginative anticipation.

82 *flowery tenderness*: fancy words of rhetorical comfort.

88 *base appliances*: dishonourable expedients.

89 *settled*: composed, immovable.

90–1 *Nips . . . fowl*: preys like a falcon on the follies of youth.

90 *enew*: trap.

92 *His filth . . . cast*: if all the foulness inside him were emptied out.

93, 96 *prenzie*: precisian (= puritan), priggish; Shakespeare's word is his own coinage—but compare *1*, 3, 51, 'Lord Angelo is precise'.

94–6 *'tis . . . guards*: it's the craftiness of hell to dress up its most damnable followers with outward trimmings ('guards') of puritanism.

100 *So . . . still*: to go on sinning in the same way.

Isabella
Oh, were it but my life
I'd throw it down for your deliverance
As frankly as a pin.

Claudio
Thanks, dear Isabel.

Isabella
Be ready, Claudio, for your death tomorrow.

Claudio
Yes. Has he affections in him,
That thus can make him bite the law by th'nose
When he would force it? Sure it is no sin,
Or of the deadly seven it is the least.

Isabella
Which is the least?

Claudio
If it were damnable, he, being so wise,
Why would he for the momentary trick
Be perdurably fin'd? Oh Isabel!

Isabella
What says my brother?

Claudio
Death is a fearful thing.

Isabella
And shamed life a hateful.

Claudio
Ay, but to die and go we know not where,
To lie in cold obstruction and to rot,
This sensible warm motion to become
A kneaded clod, and the delighted spirit
To bathe in fiery floods or to reside
In thrilling region of thick-ribb'd ice,
To be imprison'd in the viewless winds
And blown with restless violence round about
The pendent world, or to be worse than worst
Of those that lawless and incertain thought
Imagine howling; 'tis too horrible.
The weariest and most loathed worldly life
That age, ache, penury, and imprisonment
Can lay on nature, is a paradise
To what we fear of death.

105 *frankly*: freely, readily.

107 *affections*: desires.

108 *bite . . . nose*: treat the law with contempt.

110 *the deadly seven*: Roman Catholic doctrine identifies seven particular sins which are punishable by eternal damnation.

113 *momentary trick*: moment of madness.

114 *perdurably fin'd*: everlastingly punished.

117 *shamed*: shamèd.

119 *To lie . . . rot*: Claudio envisages himself trapped in his own dead body and in the grave.

120 *This . . . motion*: this living body that can move and feel.

121–8 *the delighted spirit . . . howling*: Claudio's horror attempts, with increasing hysteria, to picture to himself the condition of his disembodied spirit.

122 *fiery floods*: A river of fire (Phlegethon) surrounded the kingdom of the dead in classical mythology.

123 *thrilling*: piercingly cold.

126 *The pendent world*: the world as it floats in space.

126–8 *worse . . . howling*: worse even than the worst of those that deranged minds imagine howling in hell.

129 *loathed*: loathèd.

Isabella

Alas, alas.

Claudio

Sweet sister, let me live.
What sin you do to save a brother's life,
Nature dispenses with the deed so far
That it becomes a virtue.

Isabella

Oh, you beast!
Oh faithless coward, oh dishonest wretch!
Wilt thou be made a man out of my vice?
Is't not a kind of incest to take life
From thine own sister's shame? What should I think?
Heaven shield my mother played my father fair,
For such a warped slip of wilderness
Ne'er issued from his blood. Take my defiance,
Die, perish. Might but my bending down
Reprieve thee from thy fate, it should proceed.
I'll pray a thousand prayers for thy death,
No word to save thee.

Claudio

Nay hear me, Isabel.

Isabella

Oh, fie, fie, fie!
Thy sin's not accidental, but a trade.
Mercy to thee would prove itself a bawd,
'Tis best that thou diest quickly.

Claudio

Oh hear me, Isabella.

Duke

[*Coming from concealment*] Vouchsafe a word, young sister, but one word.

Isabella

What is your will?

Duke

Might you dispense with your leisure, I would by and by have some speech with you: the satisfaction I would require is likewise your own benefit.

Isabella

I have no superfluous leisure, my stay must be stolen out of other affairs—but I will attend you a while.

135 *dispenses*: makes allowance for.

136 *beast*: inhuman creature devoid of soul.

138 *made a man*: given life.

141 *shield*: ensure, grant that.

142 *warped . . . wilderness*: warpèd; deformed shoot of wild stock (Isabella's metaphor is horticultural).

150 *Mercy . . . bawd*: mercy for you would mean more fornication.

154 *dispense with*: give up.

155–6 *the satisfaction . . . benefit*: what I would ask from you is also for your own benefit.

158 *attend*: listen to.

Duke

[*To* Claudio] Son, I have overheard what hath passed between you and your sister. Angelo had never the purpose to corrupt her; only he hath made an assay of her virtue, to practise his judgement with the disposition of natures. She, having the truth of honour in her, hath made him that gracious denial which he is most glad to receive. I am confessor to Angelo and I know this to be true, therefore prepare yourself to death. Do not satisfy your resolution with hopes that are fallible, tomorrow you must die: go to your knees and make ready.

Claudio

Let me ask my sister pardon. I am so out of love with life that I will sue to be rid of it.

Duke

Hold you there. Farewell. Provost, a word with you.

Provost

[*Coming from concealment*] What's your will, father?

Duke

That now you are come, you will be gone: leave me a while with the maid; my mind promises, with my habit, no loss shall touch her by my company.

Provost

In good time. [*Exit* Provost *and* Claudio

Duke

[*To* Isabella] The hand that hath made you fair hath made you good: the goodness that is cheap in beauty makes beauty brief in goodness; but grace, being the soul of your complexion, shall keep the body of it ever fair. The assault that Angelo hath made to you, fortune hath conveyed to my understanding, and but that frailty hath examples for his falling, I should wonder at Angelo. How will you do to content this substitute and to save your brother?

Isabella

I am now going to resolve him. I had rather my brother die by the law than my son should be unlawfully born; but oh, how much is the good duke deceived in Angelo! If ever he return and I can speak to him, I will open my lips in vain or discover his government.

161 *assay*: test.
163 *disposition of natures*: way people behave.
164 *gracious*: virtuous.
168 *fallible*: liable to be deceived.
175 *habit*: friar's dress.
177 *In good time*: so be it.
179–80 *the goodness . . . goodness*: The duke's enigmatic observation probably means something like 'goodness that is only skin-deep in beauty will not keep that beauty for long'.
181 *complexion*: nature, make-up (spiritual as well as physical).
184 *examples*: precedents.
187 *resolve him*: let him know my decision.
191 *discover*: expose.

Duke

That shall not be much amiss, yet as the matter now stands he will avoid your accusation: he made trial of you only. Therefore fasten your ear on my advisings, to the love I have in doing good. A remedy presents itself. I do make myself believe that you may most uprighteously do a poor wronged lady a merited benefit, redeem your brother from the angry law, do no stain to your own gracious person, and much please the absent duke, if peradventure he shall ever return to have hearing of this business.

Isabella

Let me hear you speak farther; I have spirit to do any thing that appears not foul in the truth of my spirit.

Duke

Virtue is bold, and goodness never fearful. Have you not heard speak of Mariana, the sister of Frederick the great soldier who miscarried at sea?

Isabella

I have heard of the lady, and good words went with her name.

Duke

She should this Angelo have married—was affianced to her oath, and the nuptial appointed; between which time of the contract, and limit of the solemnity, her brother Frederick was wrecked at sea, having in that perished vessel the dowry of his sister. But mark how heavily this befell to the poor gentlewoman: there she lost a noble and renowned brother, in his love toward her ever most kind and natural; with him the portion and sinew of her fortune, her marriage dowry; with both, her combinate husband, this well-seeming Angelo.

Isabella

Can this be so? Did Angelo so leave her?

Duke

Left her in her tears, and dried not one of them with his comfort; swallowed his vows whole, pretending in her discoveries of dishonour: in few, bestowed her on her own lamentation, which she yet wears for his sake; and

193 *avoid*: deny, refute.

197–8 *merited benefit*: a good turn that she deserves.

206 *miscarried*: a) failed in an enterprise; b) was lost.

209–10 *affianced . . . oath*: formally contracted by oath (a contract which should have been binding on both parties—see *5*, 1, 207–8).

210 *nuptial appointed*: wedding day fixed.

211 *limit . . . solemnity*: day set for solemnizing the marriage.

216 *kind and natural*: affectionate with brotherly love.

portion and sinew: i.e. sinewy portion, effectually the strongest part.

218 *combinate*: betrothed, promised; the word is Shakespeare's coinage.

222–3 *pretending . . . dishonour*: claiming to have found evidence of her unchastity.

223 *bestowed her on*: gave her over to.

224 *wears*: endures.

he, a marble to her tears, is washed with them, but relents not.

Isabella

What a merit were it in death to take this poor maid from the world! What corruption in this life, that it will let this man live? But how out of this can she avail?

Duke

It is a rupture that you may easily heal, and the cure of it not only saves your brother but keeps you from dishonour in doing it.

Isabella

Show me how, good father.

Duke

This fore-named maid hath yet in her the continuance of her first affection. His unjust unkindness, that in all reason should have quenched her love, hath like an impediment in the current made it more violent and unruly. Go you to Angelo, answer his requiring with a plausible obedience, agree with his demands to the point, only refer yourself to this advantage: first, that your stay with him may not be long; that the time may have all shadow and silence in it; and the place answer to convenience. This being granted in course, and now follows all: we shall advise this wronged maid to stead up your appointment, go in your place. If the encounter acknowledge itself hereafter, it may compel him to her recompense; and here, by this, is your brother saved, your honour untainted, the poor Mariana advantaged, and the corrupt deputy scaled. The maid will I frame and make fit for his attempt; if you think well to carry this, as you may, the doubleness of the benefit defends the deceit from reproof. What think you of it?

Isabella

The image of it gives me content already, and I trust it will grow to a most prosperous perfection.

Duke

It lies much in your holding up. Haste you speedily to Angelo. If for this night he entreat you to his bed, give him promise of satisfaction. I will presently to Saint Luke's; there at the moated grange resides this dejected

229 *avail*: benefit.

239–40 *to the point*: in every last degree, punctiliously.

240 *refer . . . advantage*: insist on these conditions for your own sake.

244–5 *stead . . . appointment*: keep the appointment instead of you.

246 *acknowledge itself*: make itself known in public.

249 *scaled*: weighed in the scales of justice, called to account.
frame: prepare.

251 *doubleness . . . benefit*: the benefit to both Mariana and Isabella.

255 *lies much . . . up*: depends very much on your ability to carry it out.

257 *presently*: immediately.

258 *moated grange*: farmhouse surrounded by a moat or ditch.

261s.d. *Exit*: It is usual to mark scene division here, although the duke remains on stage and what follows is a continuation of the first scene's action.

Mariana; at that place call upon me, and dispatch with Angelo, that it may be quickly.

Isabella

I thank you for this comfort. Fare you well, good father.

[*Exit*

Act 3 Scene 2

The 'friar' encounters Pompey, and hears Lucio slandering the duke; he meets Mistress Overdone, discusses the state of the world with Escalus, and outlines his next scheme to the audience.

0s.d. *Enter . . . Officers*: This scene division is generally marked by editors for the convenience of readers; the duke remains on stage at the end of the previous scene.

3 *drink . . . bastard*: i.e. beget illegitimate children of different complexions; 'bastard' is a sweet Spanish wine.

5 *two usuries*: prostitution and moneylending.

Scene 2

The prison: enter Elbow, Pompey, *and* Officers

Elbow

Nay, if there be no remedy for it, but that you will needs buy and sell men and women like beasts, we shall have all the world drink brown and white bastard.

Duke

Oh heavens, what stuff is here.

Pompey

'Twas never merry world since, of two usuries, the merriest was put down and the worser allowed by order of law—a furred gown to keep him warm, and furred with fox and lamb-skins too, to signify that craft, being richer than innocency, stands for the facing.

Elbow

Come your way, sir—bless you, good father friar.

Duke

And you, good brother father. What offence hath this man made you, sir?

Elbow

Marry, sir, he hath offended the law; and, sir, we take him to be a thief, too, sir, for we have found upon him, sir, a strange pick-lock, which we have sent to the deputy.

Duke

Fie, sirrah, a bawd, a wicked bawd!
The evil that thou causest to be done,
That is thy means to live. Do thou but think
What 'tis to cram a maw or clothe a back
From such a filthy vice; say to thyself,
'From their abominable and beastly touches
I drink, I eat, array myself, and live.'
Canst thou believe thy living is a life,
So stinkingly depending? Go mend, go mend.

Pompey

Indeed, it does stink in some sort, sir, but yet, sir, I would prove—

Duke

Nay, if the devil have given thee proofs for sin
Thou wilt prove his. Take him to prison, officer,
Correction and instruction must both work
Ere this rude beast will profit.

Elbow

He must before the deputy, sir, he has given him warning: the deputy cannot abide a whoremaster. If he be a whoremonger and comes before him, he were as good go a mile on his errand.

Duke

That we were all, as some would seem to be,
From our faults, as faults from seeming, free.

Enter Lucio

9 *stands . . . facing*: sanctions the deceit ('facing' = decorative trimming).

15 *pick-lock*: skeleton key; this is never mentioned again—and may be Shakespeare's private joke, alluding to an imaginary thief in *Much Ado About Nothing* who is said (by that play's comic constable) to wear 'a key in his ear and a lock hanging by it' (*5*, 1, 301).

20 *maw*: belly.

22 *touches*: sexual contacts.

29 *prove his*: turn out to belong to the devil.

30 *Correction*: punishment.

34–5 *as good . . . errand*: do anything rather than that (proverbial).

37 *From . . . free*: free from our faults, as faults should be without disguise.

Elbow

His neck will come to your waist, a cord, sir.

Pompey

I spy comfort, I cry bail: here's a gentleman and a friend of mine.

Lucio

How now, noble Pompey? What, at the wheels of Caesar? Art thou led in triumph? What, is there none of Pygmalion's images newly made woman to be had now, for putting the hand in the pocket and extracting it clutched? What reply, ha? What say'st thou to this tune, matter, and method? Is't not drowned i'th'last rain, ha? What say'st thou, Trot? Is the world as it was, man? Which is the way? Is it sad and few words? Or how? The trick of it?

Duke

Still thus, and thus: still worse.

Lucio

How doth my dear morsel, thy mistress? Procures she still, ha?

Pompey

Troth, sir, she hath eaten up all her beef, and she is herself in the tub.

Lucio

Why, 'tis good; it is the right of it; it must be so. Ever your fresh whore and your powdered bawd, an unshunned consequence; it must be so. Art going to prison, Pompey?

Pompey

Yes, faith, sir.

Lucio

Why, 'tis not amiss, Pompey. Farewell. Go say I sent thee thither. For debt, Pompey? Or how?

Elbow

For being a bawd, for being a bawd.

Lucio

Well then, imprison him: if imprisonment be the due of a bawd, why, 'tis his right. Bawd is he, doubtless, and of antiquity too. Bawd born. Farewell, good Pompey. Commend me to the prison, Pompey; you will turn good husband now, Pompey, you will keep the house.

38 *His neck . . . cord*: he's going to be hanged.

41–2 *at the wheels . . . triumph*: The sons of Pompey the Great were led in triumph by Julius Caesar after their defeat at the battle of Munda.

43 *Pygmalion's images*: prostitutes; the statue he had carved was brought to life in answer to the prayers of the Greek sculptor, Pygmalion, and the myth was retold in a bawdy satiric poem by John Marston in 1598. *newly made woman*: recently seduced.

44–5 *putting . . . clutched*: having sexual intercourse with.

45–6 *this tune . . . method*: on this subject.

46 *drowned . . . rain*: hasn't the latest piece of legislation washed out the business.

47 *Trot*: mate (a familiar form of address).

48–9 *The trick of it*: how's it going.

53–4 *she hath . . . tub*: she has worn out all her young prostitutes ('beef') and she herself is undergoing treatment for venereal disease; beef was salted ('powdered') in a tub to preserve it for winter, and the 'sweating-tub' was used for the treatment of venereal disease.

57 *unshunned*: inevitable.

Pompey

I hope, sir, your good worship will be my bail.

Lucio

No indeed will I not, Pompey, it is not the wear. I will pray, Pompey, to increase your bondage: if you take it not patiently, why, your mettle is the more. Adieu, trusty Pompey.—Bless you, friar.

Duke

And you.

Lucio

Does Bridget paint still, Pompey, ha?

Elbow

Come your ways, sir, come.

Pompey

You will not bail me then, sir?

Lucio

Then, Pompey, nor now.—What news abroad, friar? What news?

Elbow

Come your ways, sir, come.

Lucio

Go to kennel, Pompey, go.—

[*Exeunt* Elbow, Pompey, *and* Officers

What news, friar, of the duke?

Duke

I know none. Can you tell me of any?

Lucio

Some say he is with the Emperor of Russia; other some he is in Rome; but where is he, think you?

Duke

I know not where, but wheresoever, I wish him well.

Lucio

It was a mad fantastical trick of him to steal from the state and usurp the beggary he was never born to. Lord Angelo dukes it well in his absence: he puts transgression to't.

Duke

He does well in't.

Lucio

A little more lenity to lechery would do no harm in him: something too crabbed that way, friar.

69 *wear*: habit, custom.

71 *mettle*: a) spirit; b) metal (= the prisoner's iron shackles).

86 *steal from*: get secretly away.

87 *usurp the beggary*: improperly take the position of a beggar; Lucio is very close to the truth of the situation, but the comedy demands that he cannot penetrate the duke's disguise.

88–9 *puts . . . to't*: punishes offences severely.

100 *sea-maid*: mermaid.
101 *stock-fishes*: dried codfish.
103 *motion generative*: puppet with genital organs.

107 *codpiece*: pouch in front of a man's breeches to hold the penis—here, the penis itself.
113–14 *detected . . . women*: accused of interfering with women.
117–18 *his use . . . clack-dish*: he used to put a sovereign ('ducat' = ducal coin) in her begging-bowl—i.e. he would pay to have sex with her.

119 *crotchets*: strange fancies.

Duke
It is too general a vice, and severity must cure it.

Lucio
Yes, in good sooth, the vice is of a great kindred, it is well allied, but it is impossible to extirp it quite, friar, till eating and drinking be put down. They say this Angelo was not made by man and woman after this downright way of creation: is it true, think you?

Duke
How should he be made, then?

Lucio
Some report a sea-maid spawned him, some, that he was begot between two stock-fishes; but it is certain that when he makes water, his urine is congealed ice, that I know to be true; and he is a motion generative, that's infallible.

Duke
You are pleasant, sir, and speak apace.

Lucio
Why, what a ruthless thing is this in him, for the rebellion of a codpiece to take away the life of a man! Would the duke that is absent have done this? Ere he would have hanged a man for the getting a hundred bastards, he would have paid for the nursing a thousand. He had some feeling of the sport, he knew the service, and that instructed him to mercy.

Duke
I never heard the absent duke much detected for women, he was not inclined that way.

Lucio
Oh, sir, you are deceived.

Duke
'Tis not possible.

Lucio
Who, not the duke? Yes, your beggar of fifty: and his use was, to put a ducat in her clack-dish. The duke had crotchets in him. He would be drunk too, that let me inform you.

Duke
You do him wrong, surely.

122 *inward*: intimate friend.

Lucio

Sir, I was an inward of his. A shy fellow was the duke, and I believe I know the cause of his withdrawing.

Duke

What, I prithee, might be the cause?

127 *greater . . . subject*: majority of his subjects.

Lucio

No, pardon: 'tis a secret must be locked within the teeth and the lips; but this I can let you understand: the greater file of the subject held the duke to be wise.

Duke

Wise? Why, no question but he was.

Lucio

A very superficial, ignorant, unweighing fellow.

131 *helmed*: steered through.

132 *upon . . . need*: if a reference were ever needed.

133 *Let him . . . forth*: let his achievements be testimony for him.

136 *unskilfully*: ignorantly.

Duke

Either this is envy in you, folly, or mistaking. The very stream of his life and the business he hath helmed must, upon a warranted need, give him a better proclamation. Let him be but testimonied in his own bringings-forth and he shall appear to the envious a scholar, a statesman, and a soldier: therefore you speak unskilfully; or, if your knowledge be more, it is much darkened in your malice.

Lucio

Sir, I know him, and I love him.

Duke

Love talks with better knowledge, and knowledge with dearer love.

Lucio

Come, sir, I know what I know.

144 *make your answer*: defend yourself.

146 *I am bound*: it is my duty.

Duke

I can hardly believe that, since you know not what you speak. But if ever the duke return, as our prayers are he may, let me desire you to make your answer before him. If it be honest you have spoke, you have courage to maintain it. I am bound to call upon you, and I pray you, your name?

Lucio

Sir, my name is Lucio, well known to the duke.

Duke

He shall know you better, sir, if I may live to report you.

Lucio

I fear you not.

Duke

Oh, you hope the duke will return no more? Or you imagine me too unhurtful an opposite? But indeed I can do you little harm: you'll forswear this again.

Lucio

I'll be hanged first. Thou art deceived in me, friar. But no more of this. Canst thou tell if Claudio die tomorrow, or no?

Duke

Why should he die, sir?

Lucio

Why? For filling a bottle with a tundish. I would the duke we talk of were returned again. This ungenitured agent will unpeople the province with continency: sparrows must not build in his house eaves, because they are lecherous! The duke yet would have dark deeds darkly answered, he would never bring them to light. Would he were returned. Marry, this Claudio is condemned for untrussing. Farewell, good friar, I prithee pray for me. The duke, I say to thee again, would eat mutton on Fridays. He's now past it, yet—and I say to thee—he would mouth with a beggar though she smelt brown bread and garlic—say that I said so—farewell. [Exit

Duke

No might nor greatness in mortality
Can censure 'scape: back-wounding calumny
The whitest virtue strikes. What king so strong
Can tie the gall up in the slanderous tongue?
But who comes here?

Enter Escalus, Provost, Mistress Overdone, *and* Officers

Escalus

Go, away with her to prison.

Mistress Overdone

Good my lord, be good to me, your honour is accounted a merciful man—good my lord.

158 *tundish*: funnel used to fill a brewer's cask ('tun').

159 *ungenitured*: begotten or born without effective genital organs.

160 *agent*: deputy.

165 *untrussing*: unfastening the ties between doublet and hose—i.e. taking his pants down.

167 *eat . . . Fridays*: enjoy his whores whatever the law; 'mutton' was a slang term for a prostitute, and eating meat on Friday was forbidden by the Catholic church.

169 *brown bread*: coarse rye bread, which quickly turned musty and sour.

171 *mortality*: human life.

172 *censure 'scape*: avoid criticism.

Escalus

Double and treble admonition, and still forfeit in the same kind? This would make mercy swear and play the tyrant.

Provost

A bawd of eleven years' continuance, may it please your honour.

Mistress Overdone

My lord, this is one Lucio's information against me. Mistress Kate Keepdown was with child by him in the duke's time, he promised her marriage, his child is a year and a quarter old come Philip and Jacob—I have kept it myself—and see how he goes about to abuse me.

Escalus

That fellow is a fellow of much licence: let him be called before us. Away with her to prison, go to, no more words.

[*Exeunt* Officers *with* Mistress Overdone

Provost, my brother Angelo will not be altered, Claudio must die tomorrow. Let him be furnished with divines, and have all charitable preparation. If my brother wrought by my pity, it should not be so with him.

Provost

So please you, this friar hath been with him, and advised him for th'entertainment of death.

Escalus

Good even, good father.

Duke

Bliss and goodness on you.

Escalus

Of whence are you?

Duke

Not of this country, though my chance is now
To use it for my time. I am a brother
Of gracious order, late come from the See,
In special business from his holiness.

Escalus

What news abroad i'th'world?

Duke

None but that there is so great a fever on goodness that the dissolution of it must cure it. Novelty is only in

179 *forfeit*: guilty, forfeit to the law.

187 *Philip and Jacob*: 1 May, the feast day of Saints Philip and James.

192 *brother*: colleague.

193 *furnished . . . divines*: provided with religious advisers.

194 *charitable preparation*: the spiritual preparation afforded by Christian charity.

197 *entertainment*: acceptance.

199 *Bliss*: blessing.

202 *use . . . time*: make use of it for my own particular purpose.

203 *gracious order*: a holy order of friars. *See*: Holy See, the Vatican in Rome.

204 *his holiness*: the Pope.

206–7 *that . . . cure it*: only the death of goodness can cure it.

207–8 *Novelty . . . request*: only the latest fancies are in demand.

208–10 *as dangerous . . . undertaking*: to be constant in any undertaking is as dangerous as it is virtuous.
208 *aged*: constant, persevering.
210–12 *scarce truth . . . accursed*: there's hardly enough honesty about to trust in friendship, and borrowing money is the curse of friendship.
211 *societies*: associations.
security: bonds, pledges.

220 *professed*: attempted.

222 *events*: enterprises, business.

224 *lent him visitation*: visited him; Escalus is beginning to speak in the duke's own manner.
225 *sinister measure*: unjust sentence.

227–8 *framed . . . frailty*: the weakness of his humanity had led him to imagine in his own mind.
228–9 *deceiving promises*: futile hopes.
229 *by my . . . leisure*: as time gave me opportunity.
230 *resolved*: prepared.

232 *the very debt*: the proper service.
233–4 *shore of my modesty*: limit of my humble ability.
235 *Justice*: the personification of the principle of justice.
236 *answer*: is in accordance with.
straitness: strictness.

request, and it is as dangerous to be aged in any kind of course, as it is virtuous to be constant in any undertaking. There is scarce truth enough alive to make societies secure, but security enough to make fellowships accursed. Much upon this riddle runs the wisdom of the world. This news is old enough, yet it is every day's news. I pray you, sir, of what disposition was the duke?

Escalus

One that above all other strifes contended especially to know himself.

Duke

What pleasure was he given to?

Escalus

Rather rejoicing to see another merry, than merry at anything which professed to make him rejoice. A gentleman of all temperance. But leave we him to his events, with a prayer they may prove prosperous, and let me desire to know how you find Claudio prepared. I am made to understand that you have lent him visitation.

Duke

He professes to have received no sinister measure from his judge, but most willingly humbles himself to the determination of justice; yet had he framed to himself, by the instruction of his frailty, many deceiving promises of life, which I by my good leisure have discredited to him; and now is he resolved to die.

Escalus

You have paid the heavens your function, and the prisoner the very debt of your calling. I have laboured for the poor gentleman to the extremest shore of my modesty, but my brother justice have I found so severe that he hath forced me to tell him he is indeed Justice.

Duke

If his own life answer the straitness of his proceeding, it shall become him well; wherein if he chance to fail, he hath sentenced himself.

Escalus

I am going to visit the prisoner. Fare you well.

Duke

Peace be with you. [*Exeunt* Escalus *and* Provost
He who the sword of heaven will bear
Should be as holy, as severe:
Pattern in himself to know,
Grace to stand, and virtue go:
More, nor less to others paying
Than by self-offences weighing.
Shame to him, whose cruel striking
Kills for faults of his own liking.
Twice treble shame on Angelo,
To weed my vice, and let his grow.
Oh, what may man within him hide,
Though angel on the outward side?
How may likeness made in crimes,
Making practice on the times,
To draw with idle spiders' strings
Most ponderous and substantial things?
Craft against vice I must apply.
With Angelo tonight shall lie
His old betrothed but despis'd;
So disguise shall by th'disguis'd
Pay with falsehood false exacting
And perform an old contracting. [*Exit*

241 *sword of heaven*: i.e. power, deputed by heaven, to execute justice on earth.

243 *Pattern . . . know*: to know that he himself must be the pattern for others to follow.

244 *Grace . . . go*: grace to stand firm on his principles, and strength to act upon them.
stand: withstand, endure.

245 *paying*: meting out, punishing.

250 *weed my vice*: punish someone else's offence.

253–6 *How . . . things*: The duke seems to be lamenting the criminal deceptions that are practised in these times, using the most trivial means to get control over matters of great importance.

259 *betrothed*: betrothèd.

260–1 *disguise . . . exacting*: the disguised Mariana will pay with 'falsehood'—the illusion that she is Isabella—that which is demanded by Angelo, false to his position and his 'seeming'.

262 *perform . . . contracting*: fulfil a former agreement.

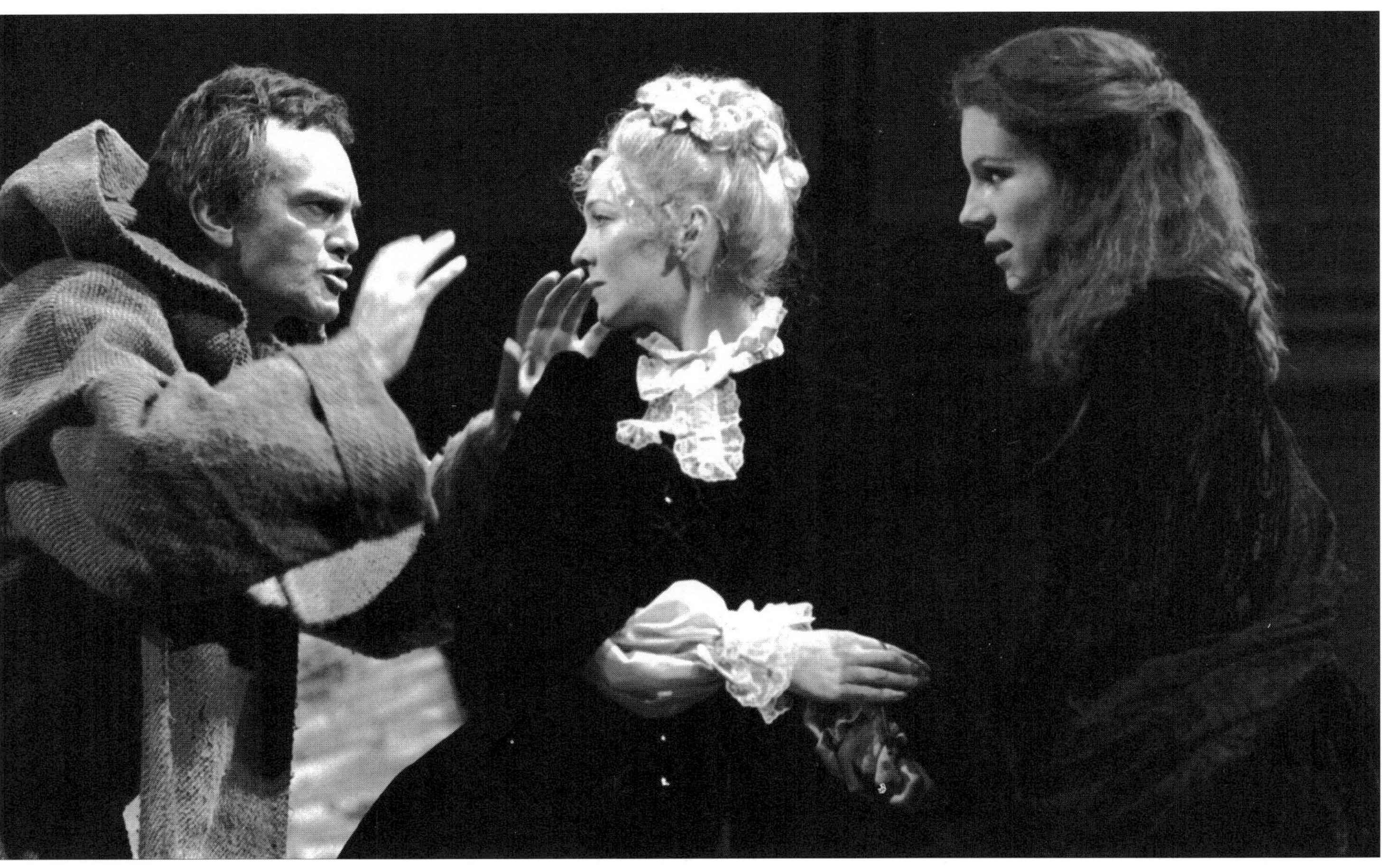

'He is your husband on a pre-contract: To bring you thus together 'tis no sin'. (*4*, 1, 71–2) Daniel Massey as the Duke, Emma Watson as Mariana, and Juliet Stevenson as Isabella, Royal Shakespeare Company, 1983.

ACT 4

Act 4 Scene 1
The 'friar' and Isabella enlist Mariana's aid in tricking Angelo.

1–6 *Take . . . in vain*: Another version of this song, with a second stanza, appears in a play by Beaumont and Fletcher (see 'A Song for Mariana', p.111).

3–4 *eyes . . . morn*: eyes so bright that morning mistakes them for the rising sun.

9 *brawling*: troublesome.

13 *My mirth . . . woe*: it didn't amuse me, but it indulged my depression.

SCENE 1

The Moated Grange: enter Mariana, *and* Boy *singing*

Boy
[*Sings*] Take, oh take those lips away,
That so sweetly were forsworn,
And those eyes, the break of day,
Lights that do mislead the morn;
But my kisses bring again, bring again,
Seals of love, but sealed in vain, sealed in vain.

Enter Duke *disguised as a friar*

Mariana
Break off thy song and haste thee quick away.
Here comes a man of comfort, whose advice
Hath often still'd my brawling discontent.— [*Exit* Boy
I cry you mercy, sir, and well could wish
You had not found me here so musical.
Let me excuse me, and believe me so,
My mirth it much displeas'd, but pleas'd my woe.

Duke
'Tis good; though music oft hath such a charm
To make bad good and good provoke to harm.
I pray you tell me, hath anybody enquired for me here today? Much upon this time have I promised here to meet.

Mariana
You have not been enquired after: I have sat here all day.

Enter Isabella

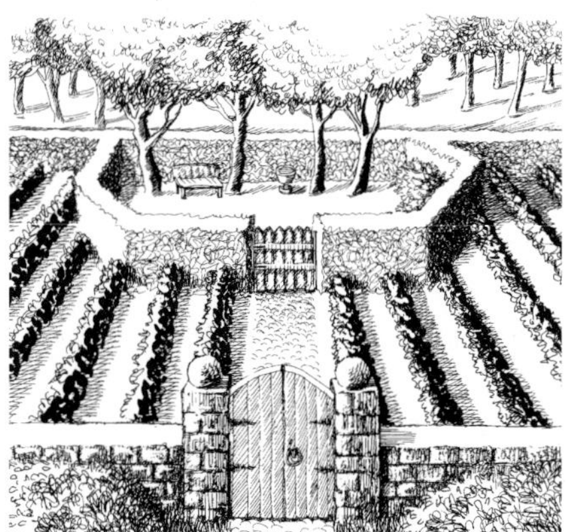

26 *circummur'd*: walled round.
28 *planched*: planchèd; made of planks.

37 *In action . . . precept*: with gestures and instructions.

39 *her observance*: what is important for her to observe.

40 *a repair . . . dark*: that she should go there in the dark.
41 *possess'd him*: made him understand. *most*: utmost.

44 *stays upon*: is waiting for. *persuasion*: belief.

45 *borne up*: sustained, thought out.

Duke
I do constantly believe you. The time is come even now.
I shall crave your forbearance a little, may be I will call
upon you anon for some advantage to yourself.

Mariana
I am always bound to you. [*Exit*

Duke
Very well met, and welcome.
What is the news from this good deputy?

Isabella
He hath a garden circummur'd with brick,
Whose western side is with a vineyard back'd;
And to that vineyard is a planched gate
That makes his opening with this bigger key.
This other doth command a little door
Which from the vineyard to the garden leads;
There have I made my promise, upon the heavy
Middle of the night to call upon him.

Duke
But shall you on your knowledge find this way?

Isabella
I have tane a due and wary note upon't.
With whispering and most guilty diligence
In action all of precept, he did show me
The way twice o'er.

Duke
Are there no other tokens
Between you 'greed, concerning her observance?

Isabella
No, none, but only a repair i'th'dark
And that I have possess'd him my most stay
Can be but brief: for I have made him know
I have a servant comes with me along
That stays upon me, whose persuasion is
I come about my brother.

Duke
'Tis well borne up.
I have not yet made known to Mariana
A word of this. What ho, within, come forth.

Enter Mariana

I pray you be acquainted with this maid,
She comes to do you good.

Isabella

I do desire the like.

Duke

Do you persuade yourself that I respect you?

Mariana

Good friar, I know you do, and have found it.

Duke

Take then this your companion by the hand,
Who hath a story ready for your ear.
I shall attend your leisure, but make haste:
The vaporous night approaches.

Mariana

[*To* Isabella] Will't please you walk aside?

Mariana *and* Isabella *walk aside*

Duke

Oh place and greatness, millions of false eyes
Are stuck upon thee; volumes of report
Run with these false and most contrarious quest
Upon thy doings; thousand escapes of wit
Make thee the father of their idle dream
And rack thee in their fancies.

Mariana *and* Isabella *approach the* Duke

Welcome, how agreed?

Isabella

She'll take the enterprise upon her, father,
If you advise it.

Duke

It is not my consent,
But my entreaty too.

Isabella

Little have you to say
When you depart from him but, soft and low,
'Remember now my brother.'

Mariana

Fear me not.

58 *report*: rumour.

59 *Run . . . quest*: follow false scents and utter misleading reports; 'quest' = give tongue like a hound.

60 *escapes of wit*: imaginings.

61 *father*: source.

62 *rack*: distort; put on the rack.

65 *not*: not only.

Duke

Nor, gentle daughter, fear you not at all.
He is your husband on a pre-contract:
To bring you thus together 'tis no sin,
Sith that the justice of your title to him
Doth flourish the deceit. Come, let us go,
Our corn's to reap, for yet our tithe's to sow. [*Exeunt*

70 *on a pre-contract*: by a binding agreement (see *3*, 1, 209–10).
73 *flourish*: decorate, embellish; the duke uses a term from embroidery and decorative penmanship.
74 *Our corn . . . sow*: we have yet to do our share before our success is assured; a 'tithe' = the part of income (1/10th) due to the Church.

Scene 2

Act 4 Scene 2
Pompey finds new employment. The duke and the provost hope for Claudio's reprieve, but are disappointed. The duke makes a quick change of plan.

The prison: enter Provost *and* Pompey

Provost

Come hither, sirrah; can you cut off a man's head?

Pompey

If the man be a bachelor, sir, I can; but if he be a married man, he's his wife's head, and I can never cut off a woman's head.

Provost

Come, sir, leave me your snatches and yield me a direct answer. Tomorrow morning are to die Claudio and Barnardine. Here is in our prison a common executioner, who in his office lacks a helper. If you will take it on you to assist him, it shall redeem you from your gyves. If not, you shall have your full time of imprisonment, and your deliverance with an unpitied whipping; for you have been a notorious bawd.

Pompey

Sir, I have been an unlawful bawd time out of mind, but yet I will be content to be a lawful hangman: I would be glad to receive some instruction from my fellow partner.

Provost

What ho, Abhorson! Where's Abhorson, there?

Enter Abhorson

3 *his wife's head*: 'For the husband is the head of the wife, even as Christ is head of the Church' (Ephesians 5:23).
5 *snatches*: quibbles.
7 *common*: public.
10 *gyves*: shackles.
11 *deliverance*: release.

Abhorson

Do you call, sir?

Provost

Sirrah, here's a fellow will help you tomorrow in your execution. If you think it meet, compound with him by the year and let him abide here with you; if not, use him for the present and dismiss him, he cannot plead his estimation with you: he hath been a bawd.

Abhorson

A bawd, sir? Fie upon him, he will discredit our mystery!

Provost

Go to, sir, you weigh equally: a feather will turn the scale. [*Exit*

Pompey

Pray, sir, by your good favour—for surely, sir, a good favour you have, but that you have a hanging look—do you call, sir, your occupation a mystery?

Abhorson

Ay, sir, a mystery.

Pompey

Painting, sir, I have heard say, is a mystery; and your whores, sir, being members of my occupation, using painting, do prove my occupation a mystery; but what mystery there should be in hanging, if I should be hanged, I cannot imagine.

Abhorson

Sir, it is a mystery.

Pompey

Proof.

Abhorson

Every true man's apparel fits your thief. If it be too little for your thief, your true man thinks it big enough. If it be too big for your thief, your thief thinks it little enough: so every true man's apparel fits your thief.

Enter Provost

20 *compound*: made an agreement.

22–3 *plead his estimation*: argue about what he's worth (i.e. about what he should be paid).

25 *mystery*: specialist occupation.

28 *favour*: a) leave; b) face.

29 *hanging look*: a) depressed expression; b) face foreboding death by hanging.

33–4 *using painting*: painting their faces.

39 *Every . . . thief*: a thief will steal anything that belongs to an honest man; Abhorson must establish his character through his attempt to elucidate this proverb.

Provost
Are you agreed?

Pompey
Sir, I will serve him, for I do find your hangman is a more penitent trade than your bawd: he doth oftener ask forgiveness.

Provost
You, sirrah, provide your block and your axe tomorrow, four a clock.

Abhorson
Come on, bawd, I will instruct thee in my trade. Follow.

Pompey
I do desire to learn, sir, and I hope, if you have occasion to use me for your own turn, you shall find me yare. For truly, sir, for your kindness, I owe you a good turn.

Provost
Call hither Barnardine and Claudio.
[*Exeunt* Abhorson *and* Pompey
Th'one has my pity; not a jot the other,
Being a murderer, though he were my brother.

Enter Claudio

Look, here's the warrant, Claudio, for thy death.
'Tis now dead midnight, and by eight tomorrow
Thou must be made immortal. Where's Barnardine?

Claudio
As fast lock'd up in sleep as guiltless labour
When it lies starkly in the traveller's bones.
He will not wake.

Provost
Who can do good on him?
Well, go, prepare yourself—[*Knocking within*] But hark, what noise?
Heaven give your spirits comfort. [*Exit* Claudio

Knocking within

By and by!
I hope it is some pardon or reprieve
For the most gentle Claudio.

45–6 *he . . . forgiveness*: The executioner always asked forgiveness of the criminal.

48 *four a clock*: Presumably (see line 53) Barnardine is to be executed before Claudio.

51 *yare*: skilful, prompt.

52 *a good turn*: The hangman was said to 'turn off' his victims when he removed the ladder from under their feet.

57 *dead midnight*: Tension will be kept high throughout this scene by constant reminders of the passage of time.
dead: deep, full.

60 *starkly*: stiffly.
traveller: 'The sleep of him that traveleth is sweet' (Ecclesiastes 5:12); the old spelling ('travail' for 'travel') would allow a pun on 'labourer' and 'one who makes a journey'.

61 *do good on*: have any good effect.

Enter Duke *disguised as a friar*

Welcome, father.

Duke
The best and wholesom'st spirits of the night
Envelop you, good provost: who called here of late?

Provost
None since the curfew rung.

Duke
Not Isabel?

Provost
No.

Duke
They will then, ere't be long.

Provost
What comfort is for Claudio?

Duke
There's some in hope.

Provost
It is a bitter deputy.

Duke
Not so, not so: his life is parallel'd
Even with the stroke and line of his great justice:
He doth with holy abstinence subdue
That in himself which he spurs on his power
To qualify in others. Were he meal'd with that
Which he corrects, then were he tyrannous;
But this being so, he's just.

Knocking within [*Exit* Provost

Now are they come.
This is a gentle provost; seldom when
The steeled gaoler is the friend of men.

Knocking within

How now, what noise? That spirit's possess'd with
haste
That wounds th'unsisting postern with these strokes.

73 *stroke and line*: written and ruled decree.

76 *qualify*: moderate.
meal'd: spotted, stained.

78 *this being so*: i.e. because he is so self-disciplined.

79 *seldom when*: it is seldom that.

80 *steeled*: steelèd.

82 *unsisting*: unassisting, resisting.
postern: little back gate.

Enter Provost

Provost
There he must stay until the officer
Arrives to let him in: he is call'd up.

Duke
Have you no countermand for Claudio yet
But he must die tomorrow?

Provost
None, sir, none.

Duke
As near the dawning, provost, as it is,
You shall hear more ere morning.

Provost
Happily
You something know; yet I believe there comes
No countermand. No such example have we.
Besides, upon the very siege of justice
Lord Angelo hath to the public ear
Profess'd the contrary.

91 *siege of justice*: seat of judgement.

Enter a Messenger

This is his lordship's man.

Duke
And here comes Claudio's pardon.

Messenger
My lord hath sent you this note, and by me this further charge—that you swerve not from the smallest article of it, neither in time, matter, or other circumstance. Good morrow: for, as I take it, it is almost day.

Provost
I shall obey him. [*Exit* Messenger

Duke
[*Aside*] This is his pardon, purchas'd by such sin
For which the pardoner himself is in.
Hence hath offence his quick celerity,
When it is borne in high authority.
When vice makes mercy, mercy's so extended

101 *For which . . . in*: of which the pardoner is as guilty as the one he pardons.

104 *so extended*: given such a wide scope.

That for the fault's love is th'offender friended.
Now, sir, what news?

Provost

I told you: Lord Angelo, belike, thinking me remiss in mine office, awakens me with this unwonted putting on, methinks strangely: for he hath not used it before.

Duke

Pray you, let's hear.

Provost

[*Reading the letter*] 'Whatsoever you may hear to the contrary, let Claudio be executed by four of the clock, and in the afternoon, Barnardine. For my better satisfaction let me have Claudio's head sent me by five. Let this be duly performed with a thought that more depends on it than we must yet deliver. Thus fail not to do your office, as you will answer it at your peril.'—What say you to this, sir?

Duke

What is that Barnardine who is to be executed in
th'afternoon?

Provost

A Bohemian born, but here nursed up and bred; one that is a prisoner nine years old.

Duke

How came it that the absent duke had not either delivered him to his liberty or executed him? I have heard it was ever his manner to do so.

Provost

His friends still wrought reprieves for him: and indeed his fact, till now in the government of Lord Angelo, came not to an undoubtful proof.

Duke

Is it now apparent?

Provost

Most manifest, and not denied by himself.

Duke

Hath he borne himself penitently in prison? How seems he to be touched?

Provost

A man that apprehends death no more dreadfully but as a drunken sleep: careless, reckless, and fearless of what's

105 *for . . . friended*: for love of the fault, the offender is shown sympathy.

107 *belike*: it seems.

108–9 *putting on*: imposition, pressure.

116 *deliver*: explain, make known.

117 *as*: otherwise.

121 *Bohemian*: Bohemia was part of the Holy Roman Empire; see *1*, 2, 1–5.

122 *is . . . old*: has been a prisoner for nine years.

127 *fact*: crime.

135–6 *insensible . . . mortal*: oblivious to the facts of life and death, and in a desperate state of deadly sin.

137 *wants advice*: is in need of spiritual counsel.

145–6 *my ancient . . . me*: my long experience deceives me.

146–7 *in the boldness . . . hazard*: with the courage of my convictions I will take a risk on it.

150 *manifested effect*: clear demonstration.

151 *four days' respite*: The duke is allowing himself plenty of time (see line 185).

152 *present*: immediate.

155 *limited*: fixed.

162–3 *discover the favour*: recognize the face.

past, present, or to come: insensible of mortality and desperately mortal.

Duke

He wants advice.

Provost

He will hear none. He hath evermore had the liberty of the prison: give him leave to escape hence, he would not. Drunk many times a day, if not many days entirely drunk. We have very oft awaked him, as if to carry him to execution, and showed him a seeming warrant for it. It hath not moved him at all.

Duke

More of him anon. There is written in your brow, provost, honesty and constancy; if I read it not truly, my ancient skill beguiles me; but in the boldness of my cunning, I will lay myself in hazard. Claudio, whom here you have warrant to execute, is no greater forfeit to the law than Angelo who hath sentenced him. To make you understand this in a manifested effect, I crave but four days' respite: for the which, you are to do me both a present and a dangerous courtesy.

Provost

Pray, sir, in what?

Duke

In the delaying death.

Provost

Alack, how may I do it? Having the hour limited, and an express command, under penalty, to deliver his head in the view of Angelo? I may make my case as Claudio's to cross this in the smallest.

Duke

By the vow of mine order I warrant you. If my instructions may be your guide, let this Barnardine be this morning executed and his head borne to Angelo.

Provost

Angelo hath seen them both and will discover the favour.

Duke

Oh, death's a great disguiser, and you may add to it: shave the head and tie the beard, and say it was the desire of the penitent to be so bared before his death.

You know the course is common. If anything fall to you upon this, more than thanks and good fortune, by the saint whom I profess I will plead against it with my life.

Provost

Pardon me, good father, it is against my oath.

Duke

Were you sworn to the duke or to the deputy?

Provost

To him, and to his substitutes.

Duke

You will think you have made no offence, if the duke avouch the justice of your dealing?

Provost

But what likelihood is in that?

Duke

Not a resemblance, but a certainty; yet since I see you fearful, that neither my coat, integrity, nor persuasion, can with ease attempt you, I will go further than I meant, to pluck all fears out of you: look you, sir, here is the hand and seal of the duke. You know the character I doubt not, and the signet is not strange to you.

Provost

I know them both.

Duke

The contents of this is the return of the duke; you shall anon over-read it at your pleasure, where you shall find within these two days he will be here. This is a thing that Angelo knows not, for he this very day receives letters of strange tenor, perchance of the duke's death, perchance entering into some monastery, but by chance nothing of what is writ. Look, th'unfolding star calls up the shepherd. Put not yourself into amazement how these things should be: all difficulties are but easy when they are known. Call your executioner, and off with Barnardine's head. I will give him a present shrift, and advise him for a better place. Yet you are amazed, but this shall absolutely resolve you. Come away, it is almost clear dawn. [*Exeunt*

167 *fall to*: befall.

177 *coat*: habit.

178 *attempt*: tempt, persuade.

180 *character*: handwriting.

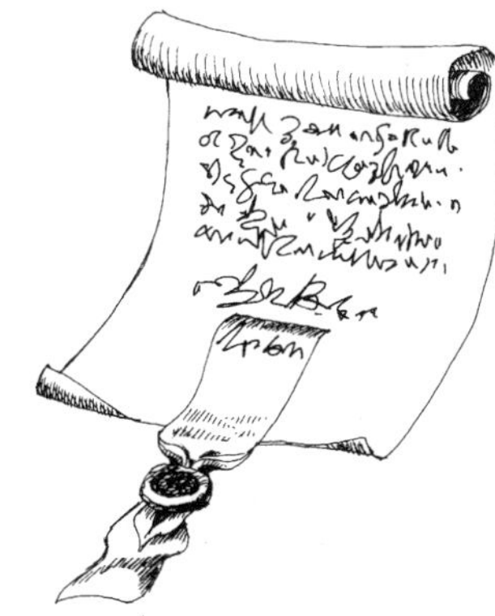

186–7 *of strange tenor*: containing extraordinary matter.

188–9 *of what is writ*: which is authoritative.

189–90 *th' unfolding star . . . shepherd*: the morning star is telling the shepherd to release his sheep from their fold.

193 *give . . . shrift*: hear his confession without delay (an essential preparation for a Roman Catholic death).

194 *a better place*: heaven.
amazed: bewildered.

195 *resolve you*: settle your doubts.

Act 4 Scene 3

Although Barnardine refuses to be hanged, a substitute is found and the duke's scheme goes ahead. Lucio tries to comfort Isabella (who thinks her brother has been executed), and continues to slander the duke.

1 *am . . . acquainted*: know as many people.
2 *profession*: prostitution.
3–4 *many . . . customers*: Pompey identifies contemporary social abuses through the generic names of his prisoners.
5–7 *commodity . . . money*: A moneylender (to get more than the lawful 10% interest) could insist that the borrower took part of his loan in some 'commodity' for resale: the goods valued at 197 pounds raised less than three pounds in cash for the imprudent Rash.
7 *ginger*: This was thought to be an aphrodisiac.
9 *Caper*: the dancer who likes to 'cut a caper'.
Threepile: the dealer in velvet (see *1*, 2, 31note).
11 *'peaches*: denounces, impeaches (with a pun on 'peach-coloured', line 10).
12 *Dizie*: the dicer.
Deepvow: the loud-mouth.
13 *Copperspur*: the man who wears fake gold spurs.
Starvelackey: the mean one who starves his servants.
13–14 *rapier and dagger*: The weapons favoured by fashionable young gentlemen.
14–15 *Dropheir . . . Pudding*: Pompey perhaps indicates a usurer who ruined a foolish heir by lending money against his prospective legacy; 'pudding' = a dull, stupid person, and 'drop' = cause to droop or pine.
16 *Shoetie*: Fashionable shoes were sometimes tied with long ribbons ending in rosettes.
Halfcan: Perhaps a reference to the prisoner's small size.
17 *Pots*: 'Potman'—bar-tender.
18 *'for the Lord's sake'*: The cry of prisoners begging alms from passers-by.

Scene 3

The prison: enter Pompey

Pompey

I am as well acquainted here as I was in our house of profession. One would think it were Mistress Overdone's own house, for here be many of her old customers. First, here's young Master Rash, he's in for a commodity of brown paper and old ginger, nine score and seventeen pounds, of which he made five marks ready money: marry, then ginger was not much in request, for the old women were all dead. Then is there here one Master Caper, at the suit of Master Threepile the mercer, for some four suits of peach-coloured satin, which now 'peaches him a beggar. Then have we here young Dizie, and young Master Deepvow, and Master Copperspur, and Master Starvelackey the rapier and dagger man, and young Dropheir that killed lusty Pudding, and Master Forthright the tilter, and brave Master Shoetie the great traveller, and wild Halfcan that stabbed Pots, and I think forty more, all great doers in our trade, and are now 'for the Lord's sake'.

Enter Abhorson

Abhorson

Sirrah, bring Barnardine hither.

Pompey

Master Barnardine, you must rise and be hanged, Master Barnardine!

Abhorson

What ho, Barnardine!

Barnardine

[*Within*] A pox o'your throats, who makes that noise there? What are you?

Pompey

Your friends, sir, the hangman: You must be so good, sir, to rise and be put to death.

Barnardine

[*Within*] Away, you rogue, away, I am sleepy.

Abhorson
Tell him he must awake, and that quickly, too.

Pompey
Pray, Master Barnardine, awake till you are executed, and sleep afterwards.

Abhorson
Go in to him, and fetch him out.

Pompey
He is coming, sir, he is coming, I hear his straw rustle.

32 *straw*: This might have been strewn on the floor, or sewn into a mattress.

Enter Barnardine

Abhorson
Is the axe upon the block, sirrah?

Pompey
Very ready, sir.

Barnardine
How now, Abhorson, what's the news with you?

Abhorson
Truly, sir, I would desire you to clap into your prayers; for look you, the warrant's come.

36 *clap into*: get a move on with, hurry up about.

Barnardine
You rogue, I have been drinking all night, I am not fitted for't.

Pompey
Oh, the better, sir; for he that drinks all night, and is hanged betimes in the morning, may sleep the sounder all the next day.

41 *betimes*: early.

Enter Duke *disguised as a friar*

Abhorson
Look you, sir, here comes your ghostly father, do we jest now, think you?

43 *ghostly*: spiritual.

Duke
Sir, induced by my charity, and hearing how hastily you are to depart, I am come to advise you, comfort you, and pray with you.

Barnardine
Friar, not I. I have been drinking hard all night, and I will have more time to prepare me, or they shall beat

out my brains with billets. I will not consent to die this day, that's certain.

Duke

Oh, sir, you must; and therefore I beseech you
Look forward on the journey you shall go.

Barnardine

I swear I will not die today for any man's persuasion.

Duke

But hear you—

Barnardine

Not a word. If you have anything to say to me, come to my ward, for thence will not I today. [*Exit*

Enter Provost

Duke

Unfit to live or die: oh gravel heart!
After him, fellows, bring him to the block.
[*Exeunt* Abhorson *and* Pompey

Provost

Now, sir, how do you find the prisoner?

Duke

A creature unprepar'd, unmeet for death,
And to transport him, in the mind he is,
Were damnable.

Provost

Here in the prison, father,
There died this morning of a cruel fever
One Ragozine, a most notorious pirate,
A man of Claudio's years, his beard and head
Just of his colour. What if we do omit
This reprobate till he were well inclin'd,
And satisfy the deputy with the visage
Of Ragozine, more like to Claudio?

Duke

Oh, 'tis an accident that heaven provides:
Dispatch it presently, the hour draws on
Prefix'd by Angelo. See this be done
And sent according to command, whiles I
Persuade this rude wretch willingly to die.

50 *billets*: little logs of wood.

53 *journey*: i.e. from life to death.

57 *ward*: section of the prison.

58 *gravel*: hard.

62 *transport*: send him to his doom.

65 *Ragozine*: a native of Ragusa, a seaport on the Adriatic coast.

67 *omit*: overlook, ignore.

72 *presently*: immediately.

73 *Prefix'd*: already fixed.

Provost
This shall be done, good father, presently:
But Barnardine must die this afternoon,
And how shall we continue Claudio,
To save me from the danger that might come
If he were known alive?

Duke
Let this be done:
Put them in secret holds, both Barnardine and Claudio.
Ere twice the sun hath made his journal greeting
To yonder generation you shall find
Your safety manifested.

Provost
I am your free dependant.

Duke
Quick, dispatch, and send the head to Angelo.
[*Exit* Provost
Now will I write letters to Angelo,
The provost he shall bear them, whose contents
Shall witness to him I am near at home
And that by great injunctions I am bound
To enter publicly. Him I'll desire
To meet me at the consecrated fount
A league below the city; and from thence,
By cold gradation and well-balanced form
We shall proceed with Angelo.

Enter Provost *with a head*

Provost
Here is the head, I'll carry it myself.

Duke
Convenient is it. Make a swift return,
For I would commune with you of such things
That want no ear but yours.

Provost
I'll make all speed. [*Exit*

Isabella
[*Within*] Peace, ho, be here.

81 *holds*: cells.

82 *journal*: daily.

83 *yonder generation*: i.e. the people who live outside the darkness of the prison.

85 *free dependant*: willing servant.

94 *By . . . form*: coolly, step by step, and with due observance of the proper forms.

98 *commune*: converse.

Duke
The tongue of Isabel. She's come to know
If yet her brother's pardon be come hither:
But I will keep her ignorant of her good
To make her heavenly comforts of despair
When it is least expected.

103–5 *I will . . . expected*: The plot demands that Isabella should not know that her brother is safe, but this explanation may damage the character of the duke.

Enter Isabella

Isabella
Ho, by your leave.

Duke
Good morning to you, fair and gracious daughter.

Isabella
The better given me by so holy a man.
Hath yet the deputy sent my brother's pardon?

Duke
He hath releas'd him, Isabel, from the world:
His head is off, and sent to Angelo.

Isabella
Nay, but it is not so!

Duke
It is no other.
Show your wisdom, daughter, in your close patience.

113 *close*: secret, hidden.

Isabella
Oh, I will to him and pluck out his eyes!

Duke
You shall not be admitted to his sight.

Isabella
Unhappy Claudio, wretched Isabel,
Injurious world, most damned Angelo!

Duke
This nor hurts him nor profits you a jot.
Forbear it therefore, give your cause to heaven.
Mark what I say, which you shall find
By every syllable a faithful verity:
The duke comes home tomorrow—nay, dry your eyes—
One of our covent, and his confessor,
Gives me this instance. Already he hath carried
Notice to Escalus and Angelo,

123 *covent*: An earlier form of 'convent'.

124 *instance*: proof, indiction.

Who do prepare to meet him at the gates,
There to give up their power. If you can pace your
wisdom
In that good path that I would wish it go,
And you shall have your bosom on this wretch,
Grace of the duke, revenges to your heart,
And general honour.

Isabella

I am directed by you.

Duke

This letter then to Friar Peter give,
'Tis that he sent me of the duke's return.
Say by this token I desire his company
At Mariana's house tonight. Her cause and yours
I'll perfect him withal, and he shall bring you
Before the duke; and to the head of Angelo
Accuse him home and home. For my poor self,
I am combined by a sacred vow
And shall be absent. Wend you with this letter:
Command these fretting waters from your eyes
With a light heart; trust not my holy order
If I pervert your course. Who's here?

Enter Lucio

Lucio

Good even; friar, where's the provost?

Duke

Not within, sir.

Lucio

Oh pretty Isabella, I am pale at mine heart to see thine eyes so red: thou must be patient. I am fain to dine and sup with water and bran; I dare not for my head fill my belly, one fruitful meal would set me to't. But they say the duke will be here tomorrow. By my troth, Isabel, I loved thy brother; if the old fantastical duke of dark corners had been at home, he had lived.

[*Exit* Isabella

Duke

Sir, the duke is marvellous little beholding to your reports, but the best is, he lives not in them.

127 *pace*: proceed, train the steps (of a horse).

129 *bosom*: heart's desire.

133 *sent me of*: wrote to me about.

136 *perfect*: fully inform.

137 *to the head*: right in the face of.

138 *home and home*: in every last detail.

139 *combined*: combinèd, strongly bound.

140 *Wend*: go along.

141 *fretting waters*: cheek-staining tears.

144 *Good even*: Lucio's greeting suggests that the time has passed very quickly since the duke's 'Good morning' at line 107.

147 *fain*: compelled.

148 *water and bran*: a frugal diet (also, apparently, a punishment for lechery). *for my head*: to save my head.

149 *set me to't*: get me going sexually, arouse me.

151 *fantastical*: whimsical, with strange ideas.

153 *beholding*: obliged.

156 *woodman*: woman-chaser.

164 *was fain . . . it*: had to deny it.

165 *rotten medlar*: prostitute; the 'medlar' (a small brown apple) was eaten only when decayed to a soft pulpy state.

Lucio

Friar, thou knowest not the duke so well as I do: he's a better woodman than thou tak'st him for.

Duke

Well; you'll answer this one day. Fare ye well.

Lucio

Nay, tarry, I'll go along with thee. I can tell thee pretty tales of the duke.

Duke

You have told me too many of him already, sir, if they be true; if not true, none were enough.

Lucio

I was once before him for getting a wench with child.

Duke

Did you such a thing?

Lucio

Yes, marry, did I; but I was fain to forswear it, they would else have married me to the rotten medlar.

Duke

Sir, your company is fairer than honest, rest you well.

Lucio

By my troth, I'll go with thee to the lane's end. If bawdy talk offend you, we'll have very little of it. Nay, friar, I am a kind of burr, I shall stick. [*Exeunt*

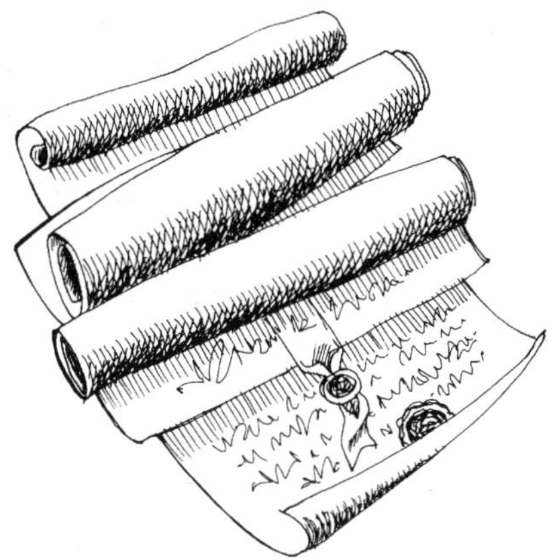

Scene 4

Act 4 Scene 4
Angelo and Escalus are bewildered by the duke's letters.

Angelo's office: enter Angelo *and* Escalus

Escalus
Every letter he hath writ hath disvouched other.

Angelo
In most uneven and distracted manner. His actions show much like to madness; pray heaven his wisdom be not tainted. And why meet him at the gates, and redeliver our authorities there?

Escalus
I guess not.

Angelo
And why should we proclaim it in an hour before his entering, that if any crave redress of injustice they should exhibit their petitions in the street?

Escalus
He shows his reason for that: to have a dispatch of complaints, and to deliver us from devices hereafter, which shall then have no power to stand against us.

Angelo
Well; I beseech you let it be proclaimed betimes i'th'morn. I'll call you at your house. Give notice to such men of sort and suit as are to meet him.

Escalus
I shall, sir, fare you well.

1 *disvouched*: contradicted.

4 *tainted*: infected with disease.
at the gates: The duke's first plan had been to meet at the 'consecrated fount' (*4*, 3, 92).

7 *in an hour*: a full hour.

9 *exhibit*: formally present.

11 *devices*: contrived plots, false charges.

13 *betimes*: early.

15 *sort and suit*: rank and following.

18 *This deed*: i.e. what he supposes to have been the rape of Isabella.
unshapes: destroys.
unpregnant: apathetic (the opposite of 'pregnant' = resourceful).

21 *it*: i.e. fornication.

23 *tongue*: speak of, denounce.
dares her no: frightens her into saying nothing.

24 *credent bulk*: weight of conviction.

27 *sense*: awareness.

32 *would . . . would not*: Angelo perhaps recalls words from the Bible: 'For the good that I would I do not: but the evil which I would not, that I do' (Romans 7:19).

Angelo
Good night. [*Exit* Escalus
This deed unshapes me quite, makes me unpregnant
And dull to all proceedings. A deflower'd maid,
And by an eminent body that enforc'd
The law against it? But that her tender shame
Will not proclaim against her maiden loss,
How might she tongue me? Yet reason dares her no;
For my authority bears of a credent bulk,
That no particular scandal once can touch
But it confounds the breather. He should have liv'd,
Save that his riotous youth with dangerous sense
Might in the times to come have tane revenge
By so receiving a dishonour'd life
With ransom of such shame. Would yet he had liv'd.
Alack, when once our grace we have forgot,
Nothing goes right: we would, and we would not.
[*Exit*

Act 4 Scene 5
The duke makes more plans.

1 *deliver me*: deliver for me.

3 *keep*: follow.

4 *drift*: intention, plan.

5 *blench*: swerve, deviate.

6 *cause . . . minister*: opportunity provides.

6–8 *Flavius . . . Crassus*: There are no speaking parts for characters with such Latin names.

Scene 5

The Friary: enter Duke, *in his own robes, and* Friar Peter

Duke
These letters at fit time deliver me.
The provost knows our purpose and our plot.
The matter being afoot, keep your instruction
And hold you ever to our special drift,
Though sometimes you do blench from this to that
As cause doth minister. Go call at Flavius' house,
And tell him where I stay; give the like notice
To Valencius, Rowland, and to Crassus,
And bid them bring the trumpets to the gate.
But send me Flavius first.

Friar Peter
It shall be speeded well
[*Exit*

Enter Varrius

Duke
I thank thee, Varrius, thou hast made good haste.
Come, we will walk, there's other of our friends
Will greet us here anon, my gentle Varrius. [*Exeunt*

Scene 6

Act 4 Scene 6
Isabella and Mariana discuss their instructions.

The Moated Grange: enter Isabella *and* Mariana

Isabella
To speak so indirectly I am loath;
I would say the truth, but to accuse him so
That is your part, yet I am advis'd to do it:
He says, to veil full purpose.

Mariana
Be rul'd by him.

Isabella
Besides, he tells me that if peradventure
He speak against me on the adverse side
I should not think it strange, for 'tis a physic
That's bitter to sweet end.

Enter Friar Peter

Mariana
I would Friar Peter—

Isabella
Oh peace, the friar is come.

Friar Peter
Come, I have found you out a stand most fit,
Where you may have such vantage on the duke
He shall not pass you. Twice have the trumpets sounded.
The generous and gravest citizens
Have hent the gates, and very near upon
The duke is ent'ring; therefore hence, away. [*Exeunt*

1 *indirectly*: inaccurately; Isabella (it seems) must allow Angelo to continue thinking he has raped her.

4 *to veil . . . purpose*: to conceal the full plan.

10 *stand*: place to stand.

13 *generous*: highly born (from Latin *generosus*).

14 *hent the gates*: taken up their positions at the gates.

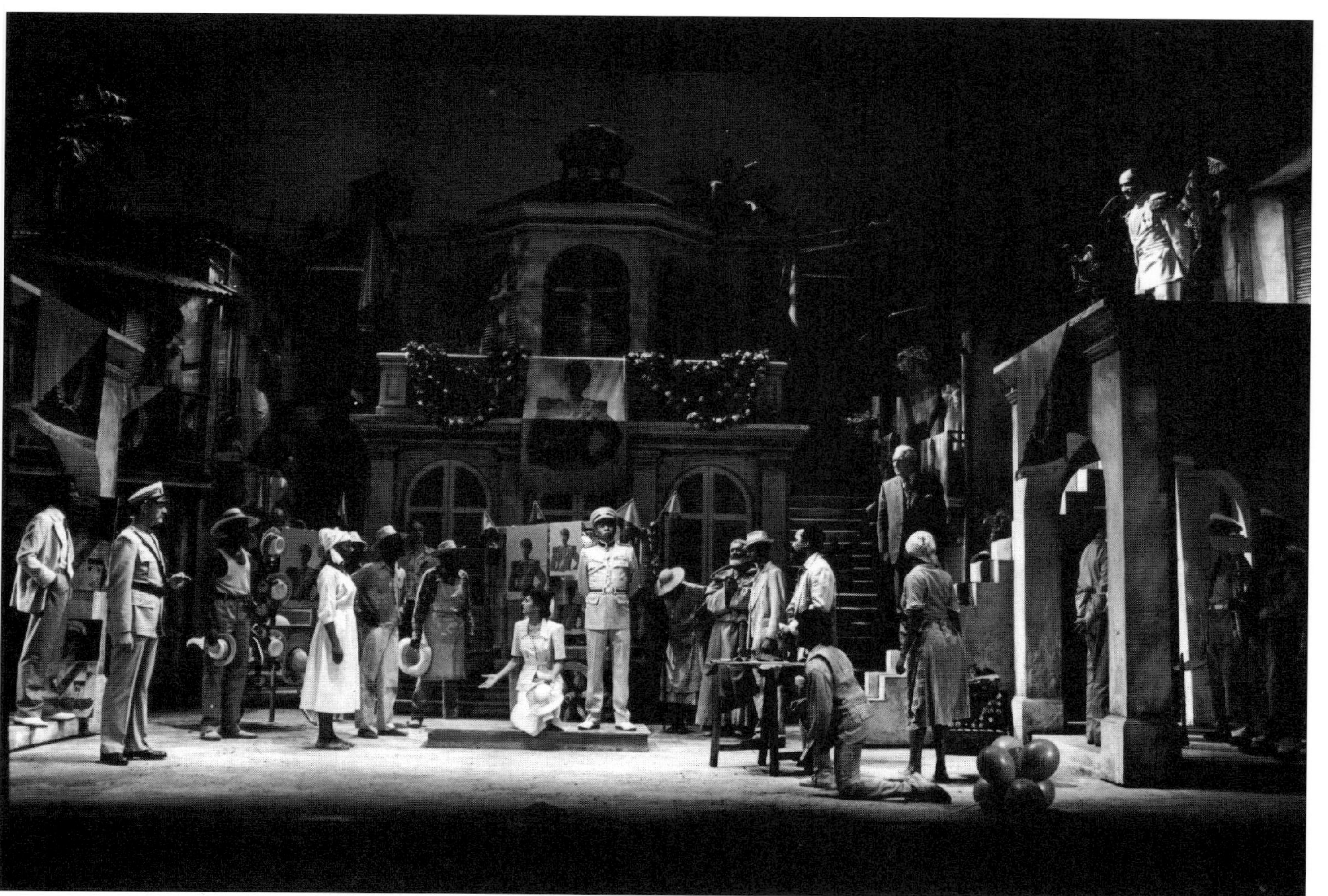

'Sweet Isabel, do yet but kneel by me'. (*5*, 1, 433) National Theatre, 1981.

ACT 5

Act 5 Scene 1
The duke, making a ceremonial entry into Vienna, hears Isabella's accusations but pretends not to believe her. She is sent to prison—and the duke disappears. Escalus will not believe Mariana until she shows her face; Lucio repeats his slanders—and discovers his mistake. Angelo confesses all; Mariana and Isabella plead for his life, and he is reprieved when Claudio reappears. Lucio is condemned to matrimony!

0s.d. *at several doors*: from different directions.
1 *cousin*: An intimate form of address—perhaps intended with (deceptive) flattery.
7–8 *yield . . . requital*: allow you to receive the public thanks before I myself give you further reward.
8 *bonds*: obligations.
10 *lock . . . bosom*: keep it locked away in the secrecy of my heart.
11 *characters*: letters.
12 *forted*: fortified.
13 *razure*: eradication, erasure.
14 *the subject*: the subject citizens.
16 *keep*: dwell.
18 *supporters*: heraldic figures supporting or standing beside a shield; the duke is presenting himself as the personification of Justice.

Scene 1

The city gates: enter Duke, *in his own robes,* Varrius, Lords, Angelo, Escalus, Lucio, Provost, Officers, Citizens, *at several doors*

Duke
My very worthy cousin, fairly met.
Our old and faithful friend, we are glad to see you.

Angelo and Escalus
Happy return be to your royal grace.

Duke
Many and hearty thankings to you both:
We have made enquiry of you, and we hear
Such goodness of your justice that our soul
Cannot but yield you forth to public thanks
Forerunning more requital.

Angelo
You make my bonds still greater.

Duke
Oh, your desert speaks loud, and I should wrong it
To lock it in the wards of covert bosom
When it deserves with characters of brass
A forted residence 'gainst the tooth of time
And razure of oblivion. Give me your hand
And let the subject see, to make them know
That outward courtesies would fain proclaim
Favours that keep within. Come, Escalus,
You must walk by us on our other hand:
And good supporters are you.

Enter Friar Peter *and* Isabella

Friar Peter
Now is your time. Speak loud, and kneel before him.

20 *Vail your regard*: look down.

28 *Reveal yourself*: disclose your complaint.

46 *th'end of reck'ning*: to the ultimate degree, absolutely.

Isabella

Justice, oh royal duke! Vail your regard
Upon a wrong'd—I would fain have said a maid.
Oh worthy prince, dishonour not your eye
By throwing it on any other object
Till you have heard me in my true complaint
And given me justice, justice, justice, justice!

Duke

Relate your wrongs: in what? By whom? Be brief.
Here is Lord Angelo shall give you justice;
Reveal yourself to him.

Isabella

Oh worthy duke,
You bid me seek redemption of the devil.
Hear me yourself: for that which I must speak
Must either punish me, not being believ'd,
Or wring redress from you. Hear me, oh hear me, here!

Angelo

My lord, her wits I fear me are not firm;
She hath been a suitor to me for her brother
Cut off by course of justice.

Isabella

By course of justice!

Angelo

And she will speak most bitterly and strange.

Isabella

Most strange, but yet most truly will I speak.
That Angelo's forsworn, is it not strange?
That Angelo's a murderer, is't not strange?
That Angelo is an adulterous thief,
An hypocrite, a virgin-violator,
Is it not strange, and strange?

Duke

Nay, it is ten times strange.

Isabella

It is not truer he is Angelo
Than this is all as true as it is strange;
Nay, it is ten times true, for truth is truth
To th'end of reck'ning.

Duke

Away with her: poor soul,
She speaks this in th'infirmity of sense.

Isabella

Oh prince, I conjure thee as thou believ'st
There is another comfort than this world,
That thou neglect me not with that opinion
That I am touch'd with madness: make not impossible
That which but seems unlike. 'Tis not impossible
But one, the wicked'st caitiff on the ground,
May seem as shy, as grave, as just, as absolute
As Angelo; even so may Angelo
In all his dressings, characts, titles, forms,
Be an arch-villain. Believe it, royal prince,
If he be less, he's nothing, but he's more,
Had I more name for badness.

Duke

By mine honesty,
If she be mad—as I believe no other—
Her madness hath the oddest frame of sense,
Such a dependency of thing on thing,
As e'er I heard in madness.

Isabella

Oh, gracious duke,
Harp not on that; nor do not banish reason
For inequality, but let your reason serve
To make the truth appear where it seems hid,
And hide the false seems true.

Duke

Many that are not mad
Have sure more lack of reason. What would you say?

Isabella

I am the sister of one Claudio,
Condemn'd upon the act of fornication
To lose his head, condemn'd by Angelo.
I, in probation of a sisterhood,
Was sent to by my brother; one Lucio
As then the messenger—

Lucio

That's I, an't like your grace.
I came to her from Claudio, and desir'd her

47 *infirmity of sense*: weakness of understanding.

48 *conjure*: appeal earnestly to, adjure.

49 *another . . . world*: a life after death.

51 *make*: consider.

52 *unlike*: unlikely, improbable.

53 *But*: but that.
caitiff: villain.

54 *absolute*: perfect.

56 *dressings*: robes of office.
characts: insignia.

61 *frame of sense*: rational structure.

62 *dependency . . . thing*: relationship between the parts.

64 *Harp*: insist.

65 *For inequality*: a) for apparent inconsistency; b) because of unequal social position.

66–7 *make the truth . . . true*: reveal the hidden truth and put aside ('hide') the falseness that appears like truth.

72 *in probation . . . sisterhood*: a novice in a nunnery.

To try her gracious fortune with Lord Angelo
For her poor brother's pardon.

Isabella

That's he indeed.

Duke

[*To* Lucio] You were not bid to speak.

Lucio

No, my good lord,
Nor wish'd to hold my peace.

Duke

I wish you now then.
Pray you take note of it; and when you have
A business for yourself, pray heaven you then
Be perfect.

Lucio

I warrant your honour.

Duke

The warrant's for yourself: take heed to't.

Isabella

This gentleman told somewhat of my tale.

Lucio

Right.

Duke

It may be right, but you are i'th'wrong
To speak before your time. Proceed.

Isabella

I went
To this pernicious caitiff deputy—

Duke

That's somewhat madly spoken.

Isabella

Pardon it,
The phrase is to the matter.

Duke

Mended again: the matter: proceed.

Isabella

In brief, to set the needless process by.
How I persuaded, how I pray'd, and kneel'd,
How he refell'd me, and how I replied—
For this was of much length—the vild conclusion
I now begin with grief and shame to utter.

82 *Be perfect*: know your part well (i.e. like an actor in a play).
warrant: assure, guarantee—but the duke takes up the sense 'order for arrest'.

90 *to the matter*: relevant.

92 *to set . . . by*: to cut a long story short.

94 *refell'd*: refused, rejected.

95 *vild*: vile (a common variant).

He would not but by gift of my chaste body
To his concupiscible intemperate lust,
Release my brother; and after much debatement
My sisterly remorse confutes mine honour
And I did yield to him. But the next morn betimes,
His purpose surfeiting, he sends a warrant
For my poor brother's head.

Duke

This is most likely!

Isabella

Oh, that it were as like as it is true.

Duke

By heaven, fond wretch, thou know'st not what thou speak'st,
Or else thou art suborn'd against his honour
In hateful practice. First, his integrity
Stands without blemish; next, it imports no reason
That with such vehemency he should pursue
Faults proper to himself. If he had so offended,
He would have weigh'd thy brother by himself
And not have cut him off. Some one hath set you on:
Confess the truth and say by whose advice
Thou cam'st here to complain.

Isabella

And is this all?
Then, oh you blessed ministers above,
Keep me in patience, and with ripen'd time
Unfold the evil which is here wrapp'd up
In countenance. Heaven shield your grace from woe,
As I, thus wrong'd, hence unbelieved go.

Duke

I know you'ld fain be gone. An officer!
To prison with her! Shall we thus permit
A blasting and a scandalous breath to fall
On him so near us? This needs must be a practice.
Who knew of your intent and coming hither?

Isabella

One that I would were here, Friar Lodowick.

Duke

A ghostly father, belike. Who knows that Lodowick?

98 *concupiscible*: lascivious. *intemperate*: immoderate.

100 *remorse*: compassion.

101 *betimes*: early.

102 *His . . . surfeiting*: his desires having been satiated.

105 *fond*: foolish.

106 *art suborn'd*: have been induced to give false witness.

107 *practice*: conspiracy.

108 *imports no reason*: doesn't make sense.

110 *Faults . . . himself*: crimes of which he himself is guilty.

112 *set you on*: put you up to this.

115 *blessed*: blessèd. *ministers*: guardian angels.

118 *countenance*: privilege.

119 *unbelieved*: unbelievèd.

122 *blasting*: infectious.

123 *practice*: plot.

126 *ghostly*: a) spiritual; b) non-existent.

Lucio
My lord, I know him, 'tis a meddling friar.
I do not like the man: had he been lay, my lord,
For certain words he spake against your grace
In your retirement, I had swing'd him soundly.

Duke
Words against me? This' a good friar, belike;
And to set on this wretched woman here
Against our substitute! Let this friar be found.

Lucio
But yesternight, my lord, she and that friar,
I saw them at the prison: a saucy friar,
A very scurvy fellow.

Friar Peter
Blessed be your royal grace.
I have stood by, my lord, and I have heard
Your royal ear abus'd. First hath this woman
Most wrongfully accus'd your substitute,
Who is as free from touch or soil with her
As she from one ungot.

Duke
We did believe no less.
Know you that Friar Lodowick that she speaks of?

Friar Peter
I know him for a man divine and holy,
Not scurvy, nor a temporary meddler,
As he's reported by this gentleman;
And on my trust, a man that never yet
Did, as he vouches, misreport your grace.

Lucio
My lord, most villainously, believe it.

Friar Peter
Well; he in time may come to clear himself;
But at this instant he is sick, my lord,
Of a strange fever. Upon his mere request
Being come to knowledge, that there was complaint
Intended 'gainst Lord Angelo, came I hither
To speak as from his mouth what he doth know
Is true and false, and what he with his oath
And all probation will make up full clear
Whensoever he's convented. First, for this woman,

128 *lay*: a layman, i.e. not in holy orders.

130 *had . . . soundly*: would have thrashed him; 'swing'd' is pronounced with a soft *g*.

131 *This'*: this is.

136 *scurvy*: bad, mischief-making.

137 *Blessed*: blessèd.

141 *touch*: sexual contact.

142 *ungot*: unbegotten.

145 *temporary meddler*: one who interferes in secular matters.

152 *Upon . . . request*: only at his request.

157 *probation*: proofs.

158 *convented*: summoned.

160 *vulgarly*: publicly.

161 *disproved*: disprovèd.
to her eyes: in front of her face.

179 *punk*: whore.

To justify this worthy nobleman
So vulgarly and personally accus'd,
Her shall you hear disproved to her eyes,
Till she herself confess it. [*Exit* Isabella, *guarded*

Duke

Good friar, let's hear it.
Do you not smile at this, Lord Angelo?
Oh, heaven, the vanity of wretched fools.
Give us some seats. Come, cousin Angelo,
In this I'll be impartial: be you judge
Of your own cause.

Enter Mariana *veiled*

Is this the witness, friar?
First let her show her face, and after speak.

Mariana

Pardon, my lord, I will not show my face
Until my husband bid me.

Duke

What, are you married?

Mariana

No, my lord.

Duke

Are you a maid?

Mariana

No, my lord.

Duke

A widow, then?

Mariana

Neither, my lord.

Duke

Why, you are nothing then: neither maid, widow, nor wife?

Lucio

My lord, she may be a punk, for many of them are neither maid, widow, nor wife.

Duke

Silence that fellow. I would he had some cause to prattle for himself.

186 *known*: had sexual intercourse with (the biblical sense of the word).

197 *With . . . love*: making love.

198 *moe*: more.

200 *just*: true.

203 *abuse*: deception.

208 *belock'd*: locked tightly.

209 *match*: appointment.

Lucio
Well, my lord.

Mariana
My lord, I do confess I ne'er was married,
And I confess besides I am no maid.
I have known my husband, yet my husband
Knows not that ever he knew me.

Lucio
He was drunk then, my lord, it can be no better.

Duke
For the benefit of silence, would thou wert so too.

Lucio
Well, my lord.

Duke
This is no witness for Lord Angelo.

Mariana
Now I come to't, my lord.
She that accuses him of fornication
In self-same manner doth accuse my husband,
And charges him, my lord, with such a time
When I'll depose I had him in mine arms
With all th'effect of love.

Angelo
Charges she moe than me?

Mariana
Not that I know.

Duke
No? You say your husband?

Mariana
Why just, my lord, and that is Angelo,
Who thinks he knows that he ne'er knew my body,
But knows, he thinks, that he knows Isabel's.

Angelo
This is strange abuse—let's see thy face.

Mariana
[*Unveiling*] My husband bids me, now I will unmask.
This is that face, thou cruel Angelo,
Which once thou swor'st was worth the looking on.
This is the hand which with a vow'd contract
Was fast belock'd in thine. This is the body
That took away the match from Isabel

And did supply thee at thy garden-house
In her imagin'd person.

Duke

Know you this woman?

Lucio

Carnally, she says.

Duke

Sirrah, no more!

Lucio

Enough, my lord.

Angelo

My lord, I must confess I know this woman,
And five years since there was some speech of marriage
Betwixt myself and her; which was broke off,
Partly for that her promised proportions
Came short of composition, but in chief
For that her reputation was disvalued
In levity. Since which time of five years
I never spake with her, saw her, nor heard from her,
Upon my faith and honour.

Mariana

Noble prince,
As there comes light from heaven, and words from breath,
As there is sense in truth, and truth in virtue,
I am affianc'd this man's wife, as strongly
As words could make up vows. And, my good lord,
But Tuesday night last gone, in's garden-house,
He knew me as a wife. As this is true,
Let me in safety raise me from my knees
Or else for ever be confixed here
A marble monument.

Angelo

I did but smile till now.
Now, good my lord, give me the scope of justice,
My patience here is touch'd. I do perceive
These poor informal women are no more
But instruments of some more mightier member
That sets them on. Let me have way, my lord,
To find this practice out.

210 *supply*: satisfy.

218 *promised*: promisèd.
proportions: dowry, marriage portion.

219 *Came . . . composition*: fell short of what had been agreed on.

221 *levity*: moral lightness, immorality.

230 *raise . . . knees*: Mariana probably fell to her knees in supplication to the duke (line 223).

231 *confixed*: confixèd; fixed firmly.

233 *scope*: full extent.

234 *touch'd*: injured.

235 *informal*: mentally deranged.

236 *member*: i.e. of a conspiracy.

Duke

Ay, with my heart,
And punish them to your height of pleasure.
Thou foolish friar, and thou pernicious woman
Compact with her that's gone, think'st thou thy oaths,
Though they would swear down each particular saint,
Were testimonies against his worth and credit
That's seal'd in approbation? You, Lord Escalus,
Sit with my cousin, lend him your kind pains
To find out this abuse, whence 'tis deriv'd.
There is another friar that set them on,
Let him be sent for.

Friar Peter

Would he were here, my lord, for he indeed
Hath set the women on to this complaint.
Your provost knows the place where he abides,
And he may fetch him.

Duke

Go, do it instantly.

[*Exit* Provost

And you, my noble and well-warranted cousin,
Whom it concerns to hear this matter forth,
Do with your injuries as seems you best
In any chastisement. I for a while will leave you;
But stir not you till you have well determin'd
Upon these slanderers.

Escalus

My lord, we'll do it throughly.

[*Exit* Duke

Signior Lucio, did not you say you knew that Friar Lodowick to be a dishonest person?

Lucio

Cucullus non facit monachum, honest in nothing but in his clothes, and one that hath spoke most villainous speeches of the duke.

Escalus

We shall entreat you to abide here till he come, and enforce them against him. We shall find this friar a notable fellow.

Lucio

As any in Vienna, on my word.

241 *Compact*: in league, confederate.

242 *swear . . . saint*: invoke every possible saint.

244 *seal'd in approbation*: tested and proved.

253 *well-warranted*: fully guaranteed.

254 *forth*: through to the end.

255 *your injuries*: the matters alleged against you.

257 *determin'd*: reached a judgement.

258 *throughly*: thoroughly.

261 *Cucullus . . . monachum*: A proverbial saying: 'The cowl (hood) does not make the monk'.

265 *enforce*: urge.

266 *notable fellow*: notorious rascal.

Escalus

Call that same Isabel here once again, I would speak with her.

[*Exit an* Attendant

Pray you, my lord, give me leave to question, you shall see how I'll handle her.

Lucio

Not better than he, by her own report.

Escalus

Say you?

Lucio

Marry, sir, I think if you handled her privately she would sooner confess, perchance publicly she'll be ashamed.

Enter Duke, *disguised as a friar,* Provost, Isabella, *guarded*

Escalus

I will go darkly to work with her.

Lucio

That's the way: for women are light at midnight.

Escalus

Come on, mistress, here's a gentlewoman denies all that you have said.

Lucio

My lord, here comes the rascal I spoke of, here with the provost.

Escalus

In very good time: speak not you to him till we call upon you.

Lucio

Mum.

Escalus

Come, sir, did you set these women on to slander Lord Angelo? They have confessed you did.

Duke

'Tis false.

Escalus

How? Know you where you are?

276 *darkly*: slyly, secretly.

277 *light*: wanton.

290–1 *let . . . throne*: 'Give the devil his due' (proverbial).

293 *in us*: i.e. his authority is vested in us.

296 *seek . . . fox*: The duke substitutes the crafty fox for the more usual wolf in this proverbial saying.

297 *Good night*: you may say goodbye.

299 *retort*: throw back.
manifest: obviously just.

306 *in . . . ear*: right in his own hearing.

307 *glance*: swerve.

309 *rack*: instrument of torture (which would stretch out—'touze'—the victim's limbs).

Duke

Respect to your great place: and let the devil
Be sometime honour'd for his burning throne.
Where is the duke? 'Tis he should hear me speak.

Escalus

The duke's in us, and we will hear you speak;
Look you speak justly.

Duke

Boldly at least. But oh, poor souls,
Come you to seek the lamb here of the fox?
Good night to your redress. Is the duke gone?
Then is your cause gone too: the duke's unjust,
Thus to retort your manifest appeal
And put your trial in the villain's mouth
Which here you come to accuse.

Lucio

This is the rascal, this is he I spoke of.

Escalus

Why, thou unreverend and unhallow'd friar!
Is't not enough thou hast suborn'd these women
To accuse this worthy man, but in foul mouth
And in the witness of his proper ear
To call him villain, and then to glance from him
To th'duke himself, to tax him with injustice?
Take him hence; to th'rack with him! We'll touze you

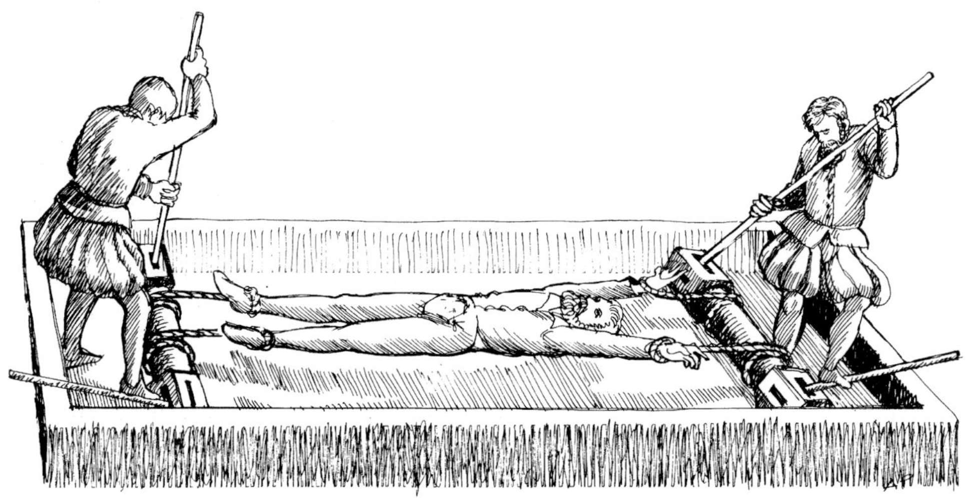

311 *hot*: hasty.

314 *provincial*: subject to local ecclesiastical jurisdiction.

317 *stew*: a) stewpot; b) brothel.

318 *countenanc'd*: connived at, protected.

319 *forfeits . . . shop*: A joke list of graded penalties was sometimes displayed in shops where barber-surgeons performed minor operations.

324 *goodman Baldpate*: 'Master Baldy'; Lucio assumes that this 'friar' has the customary shaven head ('tonsure').

330 *notedly*: especially.

331 *fleshmonger*: one who deals in flesh, a fornicator.

Joint by joint, but we will know his purpose.
What? Unjust?

Duke

Be not so hot: the duke
Dare no more stretch this finger of mine than he
Dare rack his own. His subject am I not,
Nor here provincial: my business in this state
Made me a looker-on here in Vienna,
Where I have seen corruption boil and bubble
Till it o'errun the stew; laws for all faults,
But faults so countenanc'd that the strong statutes
Stand like the forfeits in a barber's shop,
As much in mock as mark.

Escalus

Slander to th'state!
Away with him to prison!

Angelo

What can you vouch against him, Signior Lucio?
Is this the man that you did tell us of?

Lucio

'Tis he, my lord. Come hither, goodman Baldpate, do you know me?

Duke

I remember you, sir, by the sound of your voice. I met you at the prison, in the absence of the duke.

Lucio

Oh, did you so? And do you remember what you said of the duke?

Duke

Most notedly, sir.

Lucio

Do you so, sir? And was the duke a fleshmonger, a fool, and a coward, as you then reported him to be?

Duke

You must, sir, change persons with me, ere you make that my report: you indeed spoke so of him, and much more, much worse.

Lucio

Oh thou damnable fellow, did not I pluck thee by the nose for thy speeches?

Duke
I protest I love the duke as I love myself.

Angelo
Hark how the villain would close now, after his treasonable abuses.

339 *close*: get out of it.

Escalus
Such a fellow is not to be talked withal: away with him to prison. Where is the provost? Away with him to prison. Lay bolts enough upon him. Let him speak no more. Away with those giglets too, and with the other confederate companion.

343 *bolts*: fetters.

344 *giglets*: tarts, harlots.

The Provost *lays hands on the* Duke

Duke
Stay, sir, stay a while.

Angelo
What, resists he? Help him, Lucio!

Lucio
Come, sir, come, sir, come, sir! Foh, sir! Why, you bald-pated, lying rascal, you must be hooded, must you? Show your knave's visage, with a pox to you! Show your sheep-biting face, and be hanged an hour! Will't not off?

351 *sheep-biting . . . hanged*: Lucio perhaps compares the 'friar' to the proverbial wolf in sheep's clothing and threatens him with the usual penalty for sheep-stealing.

He pulls off the Friar*'s hood and discovers the* Duke

Duke
Thou art the first knave that e'er mad'st a duke!
First, provost, let me bail these gentle three—
[*To* Lucio] Sneak not away, sir, for the friar and you
Must have a word anon.—Lay hold on him.

Lucio
This may prove worse than hanging.

Duke
[*To* Escalus] What you have spoke, I pardon. Sit you down.
We'll borrow place of him. [*To* Angelo] Sir, by your leave:
Hast thou or word or wit or impudence
That yet can do thee office? If thou hast,
Rely upon it till my tale be heard,

360 *do thee office*: serve you.

And hold no longer out.

Angelo

Oh, my dread lord,
I should be guiltier than my guiltiness
To think I can be undiscernible
When I perceive your grace, like power divine,
Hath look'd upon my passes. Then, good prince,
No longer session hold upon my shame,
But let my trial be mine own confession:
Immediate sentence then, and sequent death,
Is all the grace I beg.

Duke

Come hither, Mariana.—
Say, wast thou e'er contracted to this woman?

Angelo

I was, my lord.

Duke

Go, take her hence and marry her instantly.
Do you the office, friar, which consummate,
Return him here again. Go with him, provost.

[*Exeunt* Angelo, Mariana, Friar Peter, Provost

Escalus

My lord, I am more amaz'd at his dishonour,
Than at the strangeness of it.

Duke

Come hither, Isabel.
Your friar is now your prince: as I was then,
Advertising and holy to your business,
Not changing heart with habit, I am still
Attorney'd at your service.

Isabella

Oh, give me pardon
That I, your vassal, have employ'd and pain'd
Your unknown sovereignty.

Duke

You are pardon'd, Isabel:
And now, dear maid, be you as free to us.
Your brother's death I know sits at your heart,
And you may marvel why I obscur'd myself,
Labouring to save his life, and would not rather
Make rash remonstrance of my hidden power

366 *passes*: proceedings, trespasses.

369 *sequent*: following as an inevitable consequence.

374 *consummate*: being completed.

379 *Advertising*: attentive.
holy: devoted.

381 *Attorney'd . . . service*: employed as your attorney, working on your behalf.

382 *employ'd and pain'd*: caused you effort and trouble.

384 *free*: generous.

385 *sits at*: weighs on.

388 *remonstrance*: demonstration, revelation.

Than let him so be lost. Oh, most kind maid,
It was the swift celerity of his death
Which I did think with slower foot came on
That brain'd my purpose—but peace be with him.
That life is better life, past fearing death,
Than that which lives to fear: make it your comfort,
So happy is your brother.

Isabella

I do, my lord.

Enter Angelo, Mariana, Friar Peter, *and* Provost

Duke

For this new-married man approaching here,
Whose salt imagination yet hath wrong'd
Your well-defended honour, you must pardon
For Mariana's sake. But as he adjudg'd your brother,
Being criminal in double violation
Of sacred chastity and of promise-breach
Thereon dependent for your brother's life,
The very mercy of the law cries out
Most audible, even from his proper tongue:
An Angelo for Claudio, death for death;
Haste still pays haste, and leisure answers leisure;
Like doth quit like, and measure still for measure.
Then, Angelo, thy fault's thus manifested
Which, though thou wouldst deny, denies thee
vantage.
We do condemn thee to the very block
Where Claudio stoop'd to death, and with like haste.
Away with him.

Mariana

Oh, my most gracious lord,
I hope you will not mock me with a husband?

Duke

It is your husband mock'd you with a husband;
Consenting to the safeguard of your honour,
I thought your marriage fit; else imputation,
For that he knew you, might reproach your life
And choke your good to come. For his possessions,
Although by confiscation they are ours,

391 *came*: would come.

392 *brain'd my purpose*: knocked my scheme on the head.

393–4 *That life . . . fear*: A proverbial saying: 'Better pass a danger once than be always in fear'.

397 *salt*: lascivious.

399 *adjudg'd*: condemned.

401–2 *promise-breach . . . life*: breaking the promise to save Claudio's life, which was conditional upon that violation; a double-negative construction is unintentionally misleading.

403 *The . . . cries out*: the law itself cries out in mercy.

404 *his proper tongue*: Angelo's own tongue.

406 *still*: always.

409 *deny*: i.e. that your punishment should be the same as Claudio's. *denies . . . vantage*: denies you the right to claim any better treatment.

417 *knew*: had sexual intercourse with.

419 *by confiscation*: The property of a felon was confiscate to the state.

We do instate and widow you with all
To buy you a better husband.

Mariana

Oh, my dear lord,
I crave no other, nor no better man.

Duke

Never crave him, we are definitive.

Mariana

Gentle my liege—[*Kneeling*]

Duke

You do but lose your labour.
Away with him to death. [*To* Lucio] Now, sir, to you.

Mariana

Oh my good lord! Sweet Isabel, take my part,
Lend me your knees, and all my life to come
I'll lend you all my life to do you service.

Duke

Against all sense you do importune her.
Should she kneel down in mercy of this fact,
Her brother's ghost his paved bed would break
And take her hence in horror.

Mariana

Isabel!
Sweet Isabel, do yet but kneel by me,
Hold up your hands, say nothing; I'll speak all.
They say best men are moulded out of faults,
And for the most become much more the better
For being a little bad: so may my husband.
Oh Isabel! Will you not lend a knee?

Duke

He dies for Claudio's death.

Isabella

[*Kneeling*] Most bounteous sir,
Look if it please you on this man condemn'd
As if my brother liv'd. I partly think
A due sincerity govern'd his deeds
Till he did look on me. Since it is so,
Let him not die. My brother had but justice,
In that he did the thing for which he died.
For Angelo,
His act did not o'ertake his bad intent,

420 *instate . . . you*: endow you with all a widow's rights.

423 *definitive*: decisive.

430 *in mercy . . . fact*: to pray for the exercise of mercy in the treatment of this crime.

431 *paved*: pavèd; covered with a stone (e.g. under a church or prison floor).

436 *most*: most part.

447 *o'ertake*: fulfil.

449 *no subjects*: a) not real existing things; b) not subject citizens.

460 *advice*: deliberation.

467 *still*: hitherto.

And must be buried but as an intent
That perish'd by the way. Thoughts are no subjects,
Intents but merely thoughts.

Mariana

Merely, my lord.

Duke

Your suit's unprofitable. Stand up, I say.
I have bethought me of another fault:
Provost, how came it Claudio was beheaded
At an unusual hour?

Provost

It was commanded so.

Duke

Had you a special warrant for the deed?

Provost

No, my good lord: it was by private message.

Duke

For which I do discharge you of your office;
Give up your keys.

Provost

Pardon me, noble lord,
I thought it was a fault, but knew it not,
Yet did repent me after more advice;
For testimony whereof, one in the prison
That should by private order else have died
I have reserv'd alive.

Duke

What's he?

Provost

His name is Barnardine.

Duke

I would thou hadst done so by Claudio.
Go fetch him hither. Let me look upon him.

[*Exit* Provost

Escalus

I am sorry one so learned and so wise
As you, Lord Angelo, have still appear'd,
Should slip so grossly, both in the heat of blood
And lack of temper'd judgement afterward.

Angelo

I am sorry that such sorrow I procure,
And so deep sticks it in my penitent heart
That I crave death more willingly than mercy.
'Tis my deserving, and I do entreat it.

Enter Barnardine, Provost, Claudio, *muffled, and* Juliet

Duke

Which is that Barnardine?

Provost

This, my lord.

Duke

There was a friar told me of this man.
Sirrah, thou art said to have a stubborn soul
That apprehends no further than this world,
And squar'st thy life according. Thou'rt condemn'd:
But, for those earthly faults, I quit them all,
And pray thee take this mercy to provide
For better times to come. Friar, advise him,
I leave him to your hand.—What muffl'd fellow's that?

Provost

This is another prisoner that I sav'd,
Who should have died when Claudio lost his head,
As like almost to Claudio as himself.

He unmuffles Claudio

Duke

[*To* Isabella] If he be like your brother, for his sake
Is he pardon'd, and for your lovely sake
Give me your hand, and say you will be mine,
He is my brother too. But fitter time for that.
By this Lord Angelo perceives he's safe;
Methinks I see a quick'ning in his eye.
Well, Angelo, your evil quits you well.
Look that you love your wife: her worth, worth yours.
I find an apt remission in myself;
And yet here's one in place I cannot pardon,

470 *procure*: cause.

478 *squar'st*: shape, regulate.

479 *quit*: remit.

492 *quits*: requites.

493 *her worth . . . yours*: making your worth equal to hers.

494 *apt remission*: inclination to pardon.

[*To* Lucio] You, sirrah, that knew me for a fool, a coward,
One all of luxury, an ass, a madman:
Wherein have I so deserv'd of you
That you extol me thus?

Lucio

'Faith, my lord, I spoke it but according to the trick: if you will hang me for it, you may—but I had rather it would please you I might be whipped.

Duke

Whipp'd first, sir, and hang'd after.
Proclaim it, provost, round about the city:
If any woman wrong'd by this lewd fellow,
As I have heard him swear himself there's one
Whom he begot with child, let her appear,
And he shall marry her. The nuptial finish'd,
Let him be whipp'd and hang'd.

Lucio

I beseech your highness, do not marry me to a whore. Your highness said, even now, I made you a duke: good my lord, do not recompense me in making me a cuckold.

Duke

Upon mine honour, thou shalt marry her.
Thy slanders I forgive, and therewithal
Remit thy other forfeits: take him to prison,
And see our pleasure herein executed.

Lucio

Marrying a punk, my lord, is pressing to death, whipping, and hanging!

Duke

Slandering a prince deserves it.
She, Claudio, that you wrong'd, look you restore.
Joy to you, Mariana! Love her, Angelo!
I have confess'd her, and I know her virtue.
Thanks, good friend Escalus, for thy much goodness;
There's more behind, that is more gratulate.
Thanks, provost, for thy care and secrecy,
We shall employ thee in a worthier place.
Forgive him, Angelo, that brought you home
The head of Ragozine for Claudio's;

497 *luxury*: lechery.

500 *trick*: custom, fashion.

517 *executed*: carried out.

518 *punk*: whore.
pressing to death: This was the statutory punishment for prisoners who refused to plead when they were on trial.

520 *Slandering a prince*: King James I of England (James VI of Scotland) was very sensitive to slander (which had been a treasonable offence in Scotland, punishable by death, since 1585).

521 *restore*: compensate.

523 *confess'd her*: heard her confession.

525 *behind*: yet to come.
more gratulate: more gratifying.

531 *motion*: proposition, proposal.

534 *bring*: accompany.

Th'offence pardons itself. Dear Isabel,
I have a motion much imports your good,
Whereto, if you'll a willing ear incline,
What's mine is yours, and what is yours is mine.
So bring us to our palace, where we'll show
What's yet behind that's meet you all should know.
[*Exeunt*

A Song for Mariana

Take, o take those lips a— way that so
sweet— ly were for— sworn, and those eyes, the
break of day, lights that do mis— lead the morn, but my kis— ses
bring a— gain, seals of love but sealed in vain.
Playford, bars 2-3
o take those lips a— way
Playford, bass, bar 3; bass, bar 7

The song that indulges Mariana's love-sick grief (although she seems embarrassed by its sentimentality) may well have been written by Shakespeare (*Act 4*, Scene 1). A second stanza, certainly not Shakespeare's work, was added in John Fletcher's play *Rollo Duke of Normandy* (about 1624–5), and a musical setting by John Wilson was probably composed at the same time.

I

Take, oh take those lips away,
  That so sweetly were forsworn,
And those eyes, the break of day,
  Lights that do mislead the morn;
But my kisses bring again, bring again,
Seals of love, but sealed in vain, sealed in vain.

II

Hide O hide those hills of snow,
  That thy frozen bosom bears,
On whose tops the pinks that grow,
  Are yet of those that April wears,
But first set my poor heart free,
Bound in those icy chains by thee.

The poet Tennyson was particularly sympathetic to Mariana, who is described most prosaically by the duke when he speaks of her to Isabella:

> This fore-named maid hath yet in her the continuance of her first affection. His unjust unkindness, that in all reason should have quenched her love, hath like an impediment in the current, made it more violent and unruly.
>
> (3, 1, 234–8)

Tennyson imagines the solitude and desolation of the 'moated grange' where Mariana seems to be living alone, neglecting everything as she waits without hope for the return of the man who had rejected her.

Mariana

With blackest moss the flower-pots
   Were thickly crusted, one and all:
The rusted nails fell from the knots
   That held the pear to the gable-wall.
The broken sheds look'd sad and strange:
   Unlifted was the clinking latch;
   Weeded and worn the ancient thatch
Upon the lonely moated grange.
      She only said, 'My life is dreary,
         He cometh not,' she said;
      She said, 'I am aweary, aweary,
         I would that I were dead!' . . .

* * *

About a stone-cast from the wall
   A sluice with blacken'd waters slept,
And o'er it many, round and small,
   The cluster'd marish-mosses crept.
Hard by a poplar shook alway,
   All silver-green with gnarled bark:
   For leagues no other tree did mark
The level waste, the rounding gray.
      She only said, 'My life is dreary,
         He cometh not,' she said;
      She said, 'I am aweary, aweary,
         I would that I were dead!' . . .

* * *

All day within the dreamy house,
   The doors upon their hinges creak'd;
The blue fly sung in the pane; the mouse
   Behind the mouldering wainscot shriek'd,
Or from the crevice peer'd about.
   Old faces glimmer'd thro' the doors,
   Old footsteps trod the upper floors,
Old voices called her from without.
      She only said, 'My life is dreary,
         He cometh not,' she said;
      She said, 'I am aweary, aweary,
         I would that I were dead!'

The sparrow's chirrup on the roof,
　　The slow clock ticking, and the sound
Which to the wooing wind aloof
　　The poplar made, did all confound
Her sense; but most she loathed the hour
　　When the thick-moted sunbeam lay
　　Athwart the chambers, and the day
Was sloping toward his western bower.
　　　　Then, said she, 'I am very dreary,
　　　　　　He will not come,' she said;
　　　　She wept, 'I am aweary, aweary,
　　　　　　Oh God, that I were dead!'

What the Critics have said

Samuel Taylor Coleridge

'This play . . . is to me the most painful—say rather, the only painful—part of his genuine works. . . . and the pardon and marriage of Angelo not merely baffles the strong indignant claim of justice (for cruelty, with lust and damnable baseness, cannot be forgiven, because we cannot conceive them as being *morally* repented of) but it is likewise degrading to the character of woman.'

from *Coleridge's Shakespeare Criticism*, ed. T. M. Rayser (London, 1930)

'*Measure for Measure* is the single exception to the delightfulness of Shakespeare's plays . . . It is a hateful work, although Shakespearian throughout. Our feelings of justice are grossly wounded in Angelo's escape. Isabella herself contrives to be unamiable, and Claudio is detestable.'

from *The Table Talk and Omniana of Samuel Taylor Coleridge*, ed. T. Ashe (London, 1888)

William Hazlitt

' . . . But there is in general a want of passion; the affections are at a stand; our sympathies are repulsed and defeated in all directions. The only passion which influences the story is that of Angelo; and yet he seems to have a much greater passion for hypocrisy than for his mistress. Neither are we greatly enamoured of Isabella's rigid chastity, though she could not act otherwise than she did. We do not feel the same confidence in the virtue that is "sublimely good" at another's expense, as if it had been put to some less disinterested trial. As to the duke, who makes a very imposing and mysterious stage-character, he is more absorbed in his own plots and gravity than anxious for the welfare of the state; more tenacious of his own character than attentive to the feelings and apprehensions of others.'

from *Characters of Shakespeare's Plays* (London, 1817)

Walter Pater

'The many veins of thought which render the poetry of this play so weighty and impressive unite in the image of Claudio, a flowerlike young man whom, prompted by a few hints from Shakespeare, the imagination easily clothes with all the bravery of youth, as he crosses the stage before us on his way to death, coming so hastily to the end of his pilgrimage. Set in the horrible blackness of the prison, with its various forms of unsightly death, this flower seems the braver. Fallen by "prompture of the blood", the victim of a suddenly revived law against the common fault of youth like his, he finds his life forfeited as if by the chance of a lottery. With that instinctive clinging to life, which breaks through the subtlest casuistries of monk or sage apologizing for an early death, he welcomes for a moment the chance of life through his sister's shame, though he revolts hardly less from the notion of perpetual imprisonment so repulsive to the buoyant energy of youth... Called upon suddenly to encounter his fate, looking with keen and resolute profile straight before him, he gives utterance to some of the central truths of human feeling, the sincere, concentrated expression of the recoiling flesh.' from *Appreciations* (London, 1889)

Edward Dowden 'Isabella is the only one of Shakespeare's women whose heart and eyes are fixed upon an impersonal ideal, to whom something abstract is more, in the ardour and energy of her youth, than any human personality. Out of this Vienna in which

> Corruption boil[s] and bubble[s]
> Till it o'errun the stew,

emerges this pure zeal, this rectitude of will, this virgin sanctity. Isabella's saintliness is not of the passive, timorous, or merely meditative kind. It is an active pursuit of holiness through exercise and discipline. . . . Isabella does not return to the sisterhood of Saint Clare. Putting aside from her the dress of religion, and the strict conventual rule, she accepts her place as Duchess of Vienna. In this there is no dropping away, through love of pleasure or through supineness, from her ideal; it is entirely meet and right.'

from *Shakespeare—His Mind and Art* (London, 1875)

G. Wilson Knight 'Lucio is a typical loose-minded, vulgar wit. He is the product of a society that has gone too far in condemnation of human sexual desires. He keeps up a running comment on sexual matters. His very existence is a condemnation of the society which makes him a possibility. Not that there is anything of premeditated villainy in him: he is merely superficial, enjoying the unnatural ban on sex which civilization imposes, because that very ban adds point and spice to sexual gratification. . . . He traduces the duke's character wholesale. He does not pause to consider the truth of his words. Again, there is no intent to harm—merely a careless, shallow, truthless wit-philosophy which enjoys its own sex-chatter. The type is common. Lucio is refined and vulgar, and the more vulgar because of his refinement. Whereas Pompey, because of his natural coarseness, is less vulgar. Lucio can only exist in a society of smug propriety and self-deception: for his mind's life is entirely parasitical on those insincerities. His false—because fantastic and shallow—pursuit of sex, is the result of a false, fantastic denial of sex in his world. Like so much in *Measure for Measure* he is eminently modern.' from *The Wheel of Fire* (London, 1930)

W. W. Lawrence 'Shakespeare might, after the dark shadows of the preceding intrigue, have ended *Measure for Measure* as tragedy, had he so chosen, but he determined that it should close in the spirit of comedy. The transition from the heights of tragic experience to the cheerfulness of a happy ending is too abrupt for the taste of modern critics, who like a play to be psychologically consistent. Shakespeare, however, did not shrink from violating such consistency, and executing a deliberate *volte-face* at the end. This is bitter medicine for those who claim that Shakespeare's works will appear as perfect and well-rounded wholes, if we only have the wit to look at them in the right way. We may as well admit that Shakespeare's art oscillates between extreme psychological subtlety, and an equally extreme disregard of psychological truth, in the acceptance of stock narrative conventions. To attempt to explain away the Shakespearean happy ending seems to me a hopeless task.'

from *Shakespeare's Problem Comedies* (1931)

William Empson '. . . the whole force of the case against Angelo is that, in the ordinary way, he would have been completely safe; he is a symbol of justice itself, as Escalus points out (3, 2, end); he can only be imagined as vulnerable if he is handled by very strange means. In the same way the duke's final test of Isabella, that she must forgive Angelo still believing he killed her brother treacherously, is a result of his general expectation of mercy; the fact that she agrees to it for bad reasons is not one that he is likely to realize. One might even find it pathetic that the intended nun should say "I partly think A due sincerity governed his deeds Till he did look on me". Her new sexual vanity seems meant to imply a partial awakening of her senses after the battering she has gone through; and her decision to marry the duke is perhaps not so grossly out of character as critics have supposed.'

from 'Sense in *Measure for Measure*', in *The Structure of Complex Words* (1951)

F. R. Leavis

'It is the duke who initiates and controls the experimental demonstration—the controlled experiment—that forms the action. There are hints at the outset that he knows what the results will be; and it turns out that he had deputed his authority in full knowledge of Angelo's behaviour towards Mariana. . . . The resolution of the plot, ballet-like in its patterned formality and masterly in stage-craft, sets out with lucid pregnancy the full significance of the demonstration: "man, proud man", is stripped publicly of all protective ignorance of his "glassy essence"; the ironies of "measure for measure" are clinched; in a supreme test upon Isabella, "Judge not, that ye be not judged" gets an ironical enforcement; and the relative values are conclusively established—the various attitudes settle into their final placing with regard to one another and to the positives that have been discreetly defined . . .

. . . the point of the play depends upon Angelo's not being a certified criminal-type, capable of a wickedness that marks him off from you and me:

> Go to your bosom,
> Knock there, and ask your heart what it doth know
> That's like my brother's fault. . . .

There is a wider application than that which is immediately intended by the speaker. If we don't see ourselves in Angelo, we have taken the play very imperfectly. Authority, in spite of his protest, was forced upon him, and there are grounds for regarding him as the major victim of the experiment. He was placed in a position calculated to actualize his worst potentialities; and Shakespeare's moral certainly isn't that those potentialities are exceptional. It is not for nothing that Isabella reluctantly grants:

> I partly think
> A due sincerity govern'd his deeds
> Till he did look on me.'

from '*Measure for Measure*', in *The Common Pursuit* (1953)

Classwork and Examinations

The plays of Shakespeare are studied all over the world, and this classroom edition is being used in many different countries. Teaching methods vary from school to school and there are many different ways of examining a student's work. Some teachers and examiners expect detailed knowledge of Shakespeare's text; others ask for imaginative involvement with his characters and their situations; and there are some teachers who want their students, by means of 'workshop' activities, to share in the theatrical experience of directing and performing a play. Most people use a variety of methods. This section of the book offers a few suggestions for approaches to *Measure for Measure* which could be used in schools and colleges to help with students' understanding and *enjoyment* of the play.

- A Discussion of Themes and Topics
- B Character Study
- C Activities
- D Context Questions
- E Critical Appreciation
- F Essays
- G Projects

A Discussion of Themes and Topics

It is most sensible to discuss each scene as it is read, sharing impressions (and perhaps correcting misapprehensions): no two people experience any character in quite the same way, and we all have different expectations. It can be useful to compare aspects of this play with other fictions—plays, novels, films—or with modern life. A large class can divide into small groups, each with a leader, who can discuss different aspects of a single topic and then report back to the main assembly.

A1 The Duke of Vienna believes that we have a moral obligation to use our talents for the benefit of others—

Thyself and thy belongings
Are not thine own so proper as to waste
Thyself upon thy virtues, they on thee.
Heaven doth with us as we with torches do,
Not light them for themselves (*1*, 1, 29–33)

Do you agree with him? Should this apply to states and nations as well as to individuals?

A2 A popular ruler? The duke recognizes the value of popularity—but he is mistrustful:

> I love the people,
> But do not like to stage me to their eyes:
> Though it do well I do not relish well
> Their loud applause and aves vehement,
> Nor do I think the man of safe discretion
> That does affect it. (*1*, 1, 67–72)

To what extent do you think that those in high positions—queen or king, prime minister or president, principal or head teacher—should strive for popularity among their subjects, citizens, students?

A3 Claudio blames himself for his present predicament, saying that it comes

> From too much liberty, my Lucio, liberty.
> As surfeit is the father of much fast,
> So every scope by the immoderate use
> Turns to restraint. (*1*, 2, 113–16)

When does liberty become licence? How far should the state (ruler, governor) go in controlling individual liberties? What rights have schools/teachers/parents to control the behaviour of students/children?

A4 Isabella seems content to accept double standards in language and behaviour—

> Great men may jest with saints: 'tis wit in them,
> But in the less foul profanation . . .
> That in the captain's but a choleric word
> Which in the soldier is flat blasphemy. (2, 2, 131–5)

Would you agree with her? Do we today allow greater licence to persons in the limelight—e.g. pop stars, film stars, footballers—than we would accept from ordinary people?

A5 Angelo presents Isabella with a moral dilemma:

> Which had you rather: that the most just law
> Now took your brother's life, or to redeem him
> Give up your body to such sweet uncleanness
> As she that he hath stain'd? (2, 4, 51–4)

Should Isabella sacrifice her virginity to save her brother's life? Is it ever right to do a bad deed for a good reason? Can the end sometimes justify the means?

A6 'Sweet sister, let me live': what right has a brother to make such a demand of his sister?

A7 'Slandering a prince', according to the duke (5, 1, 520), deserves 'pressing to death, whipping, and hanging'. Do you think there should be some kind of censorship on the media, the writer, and the entertainment business for the protection of royalty (and other people in prominent positions—e.g. government officials)?

A8 The duke ends the play with a proposition for Isabella—

> Whereto, if you'll a willing ear incline,
> What's mine is yours, and what is yours is mine.

What reply should Isabella make?

A9
> An Angelo for Claudio, death for death;
> Haste still pays haste, and leisure answers leisure;
> Like doth quit like, and measure still for measure.
>
> (5, 1, 405–7)

Is this *your* idea of justice?

A10 Consider the possibilities of staging this play in settings other than seventeenth-century England. Different periods? Different countries? With a racially mixed cast?

B Character Study

Shakespeare's characters can be studied in many different ways, either from the *outside*, where the detached, critical student (or group of students) can see the function of every character within the whole scheme and pattern of the play; or from the *inside*, where the sympathetic student (like an actor) can identify with a single character and can look at the action and the other characters from his/her point of view.

a) from 'outside' the character

B1 Compare the characters of Escalus and Angelo as they appear in the first scene of the play. Does it seem to you that the duke has made the right choice of deputy?

B2 'Authority, in spite of his protest, was forced upon him [Angelo], and there are grounds for regarding him as the major victim of the experiment' (F. R. Leavis): how far would you agree with this observation?

B3 'If I could speak so wisely under an arrest' (*1*, 2, 119): Claudio can sometimes put on a brave face—but underneath he is really a very frightened young man. Demonstrate the truth of this comment.

B4 'this gentleman . . . had a most noble father' (*2*, 1, 6–7): what does this comment tell you about Escalus? How effective is he as a magistrate?

B5 Although their parts are small, they are all essential to the play: discuss the character and function in the play of any of the following—

a) Elbow
b) The Provost
c) Mistress Overdone
d) Barnardine

B6 'Angelo, though morally guilty of lust and murder, and actually guilty of meanness, blackmail, and treachery, is not really a "villain"' (Kenneth Muir). What is your response to this judgement?

B7 'What dost thou or what art thou . . . ?' (*2*, 2, 177): both Angelo and Isabella are given a crash course in self-knowledge. Discuss the lessons that either (or both) must learn.

B8 Is Lucio no more than a 'typical loose-minded, vulgar wit' (Wilson Knight—see 'What the Critics have Said', page 115)? In what ways is he important to the play?

B9 'Mariana was brought into the play merely to protect Isabella's virginity: the character has no further interest or importance': how far do you agree with this statement?

B10 The duke has 'ever lov'd the life remov'd' (*1*, 3, 9). What signs of this can we find in Vienna? Is the duke the real villain of the piece?

b) from 'inside' the character

B11 A controlled experiment—and a way of killing two birds with one stone! The duke sets out his plan of action before authorizing Angelo to begin the clean-up of Vienna—and afterwards he writes a critical report on his success.

B12 In the character of either Escalus or Angelo writing a diary entry or personal letter, describe your thoughts and feelings about the state of Vienna and the present situation.

B13 The Provost carries letters (and perhaps poems) between Claudio and Juliet whilst they are in prison: compose this correspondence.

B14 Isabella writes to the Mother Superior of her convent, describing her brother and his girlfriend and saying what she thinks of the 'crime' they have committed.

B15 The trial of Pompey and Froth proves to be rather a fiasco: report it from the standpoint of one of these characters—

Angelo	Escalus
Pompey	Elbow
Froth	a journalist from the local newspaper

B16 'What, do I love her That I desire to hear her speak again And feast upon her eyes?' (2, 2, 181–3): Angelo, confiding his thoughts to a very personal diary, wrestles with his lust and his conscience.

B17 'Death is a fearful thing' (3, 1, 116): when you have read Claudio's thoughts about death and dying, try to write down your own in any form of verse or prose that most appeals to you.

B18 What does Mariana think about the 'bed trick' deception that she must perform? Write (perhaps for serialization in some newspaper) the full account of her love story from the time of the broken engagement—or even before—until she finally gets her man.

B19 By this Lord Angelo perceives he's safe;
Methinks I see a quick'ning in his eye. (5, 1, 490–1)

What are the thoughts going through Angelo's mind when he hears these words? Trace his thought processes throughout *Act* 5, Scene 1 (or some part of this scene).

B20 It would be interesting to know Isabella's thoughts and feelings on certain subjects and at certain points in the play: write a soliloquy, 'stream of consciousness' monologue, or diary/letter report for her on one of these occasions:

a) when the duke explains his 'bed trick' (3, 1, 234–52)
b) when the duke sends her to prison (5, 1, 121)
c) when Escalus is threatening the 'friar' (5, 1, 303–10)

d) when Angelo is being sentenced (5, 1, 358–75)
e) 'Give me your hand, and say you will be mine' (5, 1, 488)

C Activities

These can involve several students working together, preferably *away from* the desk or study-table. They can help students to develop a sense of drama and the dramatic effects of Shakespeare's verse—which, after all, was written to be spoken and performed, not read silently.

C1 Speak the lines—act the scenes! To familiarize yourselves with Shakespeare's verse, try different reading techniques—reading by punctuation marks (where each person hands over to the next at every punctuation mark); reading by sentences; and reading by speeches. Begin acting with small units—about ten lines—where two or three characters are speaking to each other; rehearse these in groups of students, and perform them before the whole class. Read the lines from a script—then act them out in your own words.

C2 'Let us withdraw together'. Create a scene in which Angelo and Escalus discuss the state of Vienna and examine their new commissions. Will Angelo declare his plans for a complete moral clean-up?

C3 Angelo's 'thought-police' are everywhere, and they arrest the men who were with Lucio (*Act 1*, Scene 2) to question them about their attitudes to sex, women, and sexually transmitted diseases (What do they know about syphilis? Do they care about infecting an unborn child?).

C4 In a modern democratic society, Angelo and his legislation would be subject to keen media scrutiny. Remembering that Vienna is compared (5, 1, 316) to a stewpot where 'corruption boil[s] and bubble[s]', present a televised interview with Angelo—perhaps with questions from the studio audience.

C5 Several scenes seem to open in the middle of a conversation: script and perform the discussions between some of these characters *before* they appear on stage:

a) The duke and Friar Thomas (*Act 1*, Scene 3)
b) Angelo and Escalus (*Act 2*, Scene 1)
c) The 'friar' and Claudio (*Act 3*, Scene 1)
d) Isabella and Mariana (*Act 4*, Scene 6)

C6 'What is a woman's "destin'd livery" (2, 4, 139)?' Organize a discussion panel consisting of Isabella, Juliet, Mariana, Sister Francisca, and Mistress Overdone to debate this topic.

C7 The 'friar' tactfully sends Isabella and Mariana away to '*walk aside*' and discuss the 'bed trick' he is planning: devise a scene (either in blank verse or in modern prose) for their conversation.

C8 In the modern world, the duke's return to Vienna would attract only a moderate amount of international media coverage—until a young woman breaks through the crowds and throws herself at the duke's feet calling for justice. Then it's a big story! Provide a running commentary for radio and (with signing for the deaf) television; file reports for newspapers and devise banner headlines; get interviews (exclusive) with anybody who knows anything. Could such a thing happen here? Try to get a comment from the prime minister/president/governor. What do viewers/listeners/readers at home think about these goings-on?

D Context Questions

Questions like these, which are sometimes used in written examinations, can also be helpful as a class revision quiz, testing knowledge of the play and some understanding of its words.

D1 He should have liv'd,
Save that his riotous youth with dangerous sense
Might in the times to come have tane revenge
By so receiving a dishonour'd life
With ransom of such shame.

(i) Who is speaking, and who is being spoken of?
(ii) What is the 'ransom' that is mentioned?
(iii) Has the ransom been paid? By whom?
(iv) What is the office of the speaker?

D2 A tapster, sir, parcel bawd, one that serves a bad woman, whose house, sir, was, as they say, plucked down in the suburbs; and now she professes a hot-house; which I think is a very ill house too.

(i) Who is speaking, and who is being addressed?
(ii) What is the name of the 'tapster', and who is the 'bad woman'?
(iii) What is the office of the speaker?
(iv) What is a 'parcel bawd'?

D3 Is't not enough thou hast suborn'd these women
To accuse this worthy man, but in foul mouth
And in the witness of his proper ear
To call him villain, and then to glance from him
To th'duke himself, to tax him with injustice?

(i) Who is the speaker and who is 'this worthy man'?
(ii) Who is being spoken to?
(iii) What is the occasion?
(iv) Who has made accusations against the duke?
(v) What is the meaning of 'his proper ear'?

D4 Oh, 'tis an accident that heaven provides:
Dispatch it presently, the hour draws on
Prefix'd by ——. See this be done
And sent according to command, whiles I
Persuade this rude wretch willingly to die.

(i) What has 'heaven' provided, and why is it necessary?
(ii) Who is speaking and to whom does he speak?
(iii) Who is the 'rude wretch' and what has he done?
(iv) What hour has been 'Prefix'd' and by whom?

E Critical Appreciation

These also present passages from the play and ask questions about them; again you often have a choice of passages, but the extracts are much longer than those presented as context questions. Some examination boards allow candidates to take their copies of the play into the examination room, asking them to re-read specified sections of the play (such as the one printed here) and answer questions on them.

E1 *Act* 2, Scene 4, lines 81–131

But mark me.
To be receivèd plain, I'll speak more gross:
Your brother is to die.

Isabella
So.

Angelo
And his offence is so as it appears
Accountant to the law upon that pain.

Isabella
True.

Angelo
Admit no other way to save his life—
As I subscribe not that, nor any other,
But in the loss of question—that you, his sister,
Finding yourself desir'd of such a person
Whose credit with the judge, or own great place,
Could fetch your brother from the manacles
Of the all-binding law, and that there were
No earthly mean to save him, but that either
You must lay down the treasures of your body
To this suppos'd, or else to let him suffer:
What would you do?

Isabella
As much for my poor brother as myself:
That is, were I under the terms of death,
Th'impression of keen whips I'd wear as rubies,
And strip myself to death as to a bed
That longing have been sick for, ere I'd yield
My body up to shame.

Angelo
Then must your brother die.

Isabella
And 'twere the cheaper way:
Better it were a brother died at once,
Than that a sister by redeeming him
Should die for ever.

Angelo
Were not you then as cruel as the sentence
That you have slander'd so?

Isabella
Ignomy in ransom and free pardon
Are of two houses: lawful mercy
Is nothing kin to foul redemption.

Angelo
You seem'd of late to make the law a tyrant,
And rather prov'd the sliding of your brother
A merriment than a vice.

Isabella
Oh, pardon me, my lord, it oft falls out
To have what we would have, we speak not what we mean.

I something do excuse the thing I hate
For his advantage that I dearly love.

Angelo
We are all frail.

Isabella
Else let my brother die,
If not a fedary but only he
Owe and succeed thy weakness.

Angelo
Nay, women are frail too.

Isabella
Ay, as the glasses where they view themselves,
Which are as easy broke as they make forms.
Women? Help heaven, men their creation mar
In profiting by them. Nay, call us ten times frail,
For we are soft as our complexions are,
And credulous to false prints.

Claudio praised his sister for her 'prosperous art When she will play with reason and discourse' (*1*, 2, 168–9). What does this passage show you of Isabella's powers of persuasion?

E2 Read again *Act 1*, Scene 2, lines 103–181 ('*Enter* Provost . . . Gentlemen' to 'Come, officer, away'). What do you learn from this passage about the different characters and their attitudes to authority and the social order of Vienna?

E3 Re-read *Act 1*, Scene 4, lines 16–90 ('Hail virgin, if you be' . . . 'I take my leave of you'). Are you surprised by Lucio's conduct in this scene? What other roles does he play in the course of the action?

E4 Read again *Act 4*, Scene 2, lines 62–196 ('*Knocking within*' . . . 'almost clear dawn'). Show how Shakespeare creates suspense in this scene. How important is the dramatic irony here?

E5 Re-read *Act 5*, Scene 1, lines 69–162 ('I am the sister of one Claudio' . . . 'she herself confess it'). Discuss the duke's handling of this situation.

F Essays These will usually give you a specific topic to discuss, or perhaps a question that must be answered, in writing, *with a reasoned argument.* They *never* want you to tell the story of the play—so don't! Your examiner—or teacher—has read the play, and does not need to be reminded of it. Relevant quotations will always help you to make your points more strongly.

F1 'If your worship will take order for the drabs and the knaves, you need not to fear the bawds' (2, 1, 211–13): is Pompey's the voice of commonsense in Vienna?

F2 Discuss the play's presentation of 'man, proud man, Dress'd in a little brief authority' (2, 2, 121–2)

F3 *Measure for Measure*—how apt is the title of this play?

F4 'The character that Shakespeare has created in Isabella is too intelligent, too independent, and will hardly fit into his plot: she could never wear the "destin'd livery" (2, 4, 139) that seems to be planned for her?' What truth is there in this comment? Is this a serious weakness in the play?

F5 'It is a *hateful* work . . . [and] our feelings of justice are grossly wounded in Angelo's escape': how would *you* reply to the criticism of Samuel Taylor Coleridge?

G Projects

In some schools, students are required to do more 'free-ranging' work, which takes them outside the text—but which should always be relevant to the play. Such Projects may demand skills—design and artwork for instance—other than reading and writing, and may be presented in a portfolio of work assembled over a certain period of time. The availability of resources will, obviously, do much to determine the nature of the Projects, but this is something that only local teachers will understand.

Suggested Subjects

G1 Staging the play: set and costume designs for some part of *Measure for Measure.*

G2 Isabella and/or Angelo in theatrical history.

G3 The Order of the Poor Clares.

G4 Local Government in early-seventeenth-century England.

G5 London's Bankside and Shakespeare's Globe theatre.

Background

England c. *1604*

When Shakespeare was writing *Measure for Measure*, most people still believed that the sun went round the earth. They were taught that this was a divinely ordered scheme of things, and that—in England—God had instituted a Church and ordained a Monarchy for the right government of the land and the populace.

'The past is a foreign country; they do things differently there.'

L. P. Hartley

Government For most of Shakespeare's life, the reigning monarch of England was Queen Elizabeth I: when she died, she was succeeded by King James I. He was also king of Scotland (James VI), and the two kingdoms were united in 1603 by his accession to the English throne. With his counsellors and ministers, King James governed the nation (population less than six million) from London, although fewer than half a million people inhabited the capital city. In the rest of the country, law and order were maintained by the land-owners and enforced by their deputies. It was a period of high inflation, when political and social unease presented constant threats to the king and the establishment, and when poverty was widespread. The average man had no vote—and his wife had no rights at all.

Religion At this time, England was a Christian country. All children were baptized, soon after they were born, into the Church of England; they were taught the essentials of the Christian faith, and instructed in their duty to God and to humankind. Marriages were performed, and funerals conducted, only by the licensed clergy and in accordance with the Church's rites and ceremonies—although many people (like Claudio and Juliet) were content with an incomplete contractual relationship for all their lives. Attendance at divine service, however, was compulsory, and absences (without good—medical—reason) could be punished by fines. By such means, the authorities were able to keep some check on the populace—recording births, marriages, and deaths; being alert to any religious nonconformity, which could be politically dangerous; and ensuring a minimum of orthodox instruction through the official 'Homilies' which were regularly preached from the pulpits of all parish churches throughout the realm.

Following Henry VIII's break away from the Church of Rome, all people in England were able to hear the church services *in their own language*. The Book of Common Prayer was used in every church, and an English translation of the Bible was read aloud in public. The Christian religion had never been so well taught before!

Education

School education reinforced the Church's teaching. From the age of four, boys might attend the 'petty school' (French '*petite école*') to learn the rudiments of reading and writing along with a few prayers; some schools also included work with numbers. At the age of seven, the boy was ready for the grammar school (if his father was willing and able to pay the fees).

Here, a thorough grounding in Latin grammar was followed by translation work and the study of Roman authors, paying attention as much to style as to matter. The arts of fine writing were thus inculcated from early youth. A very few students proceeded to university; these were either clever scholarship boys, or else the sons of noblemen. Girls stayed at home, and acquired domestic and social skills—cooking, sewing, perhaps even music. The lucky ones might learn to read and write.

Language

At the start of the sixteenth century the English had a very poor opinion of their own language: there was little serious writing in English, and hardly any literature. Latin was the language of international scholarship, and Englishmen admired the eloquence of the Romans. They made many translations, and in this way they extended the resources of their own language, increasing its vocabulary and stretching its grammatical structures. French, Italian, and Spanish works were also translated and, for the first time, there were English versions of the Bible. By the end of the century, English was a language to be proud of: it was rich in synonyms, capable of infinite variety and subtlety, and ready for all kinds of word-play—especially the *puns*, for which Elizabethan English is renowned.

Drama

The great art-form of the Elizabethan and Jacobean age was its drama. The Elizabethans inherited a tradition of play-acting from the Middle Ages, and they reinforced this by reading and translating the Roman playwrights. At the beginning of the sixteenth century plays were performed by groups of actors, all-male companies (boys acted the female roles) who travelled from town to town, setting up their stages in open places (such as inn-yards) or, with the permission of the owner, in the hall of some noble house. The touring companies continued in the provinces into the seventeenth century; but in London, in 1576, a new building was erected for the performance of plays. This was the Theatre, the first purpose-built playhouse in England. Other playhouses followed, (including the Globe, where most of Shakespeare's plays were performed), and the English drama reached new heights of eloquence.

There were those who disapproved, of course. The theatres, which brought large crowds together, could encourage the spread of disease—and dangerous ideas. During the summer, when the plague was at its worst, the playhouses were closed. A constant censorship was imposed, more or less severe at different times. The Puritan faction tried to close down the theatres, but—partly because there was royal favour for the drama, and partly because the buildings were outside the city limits—they did not succeed until 1642.

Theatre From contemporary comments and sketches—most particularly a drawing by a Dutch visitor, Johannes de Witt—it is possible to form some idea of the typical Elizabethan playhouse for which most of Shakespeare's plays were written. Hexagonal in shape, it had three roofed galleries encircling an open courtyard. The plain, high stage projected into the yard, where it was surrounded by the audience of standing 'groundlings'. At the back were two doors for the actors' entrances and exits, and between these doors was a curtained 'discovery space' (sometimes called an 'inner stage'). Above this was a balcony, used as a musicians' gallery or for the performance of scenes 'above', and projecting over part of the stage was a roof, supported on two pillars, which was painted with the sun, moon, and stars for the 'heavens'.

Underneath was space (concealed by curtaining) which could be used by characters ascending and descending through a trap-door in the stage. Costumes and properties were kept backstage in the 'tiring house'. The actors dressed lavishly, often wearing the secondhand clothes bestowed by rich patrons. Stage properties were important for defining a location, but the dramatist's own words were needed to explain the time of day, since all performances took place in the early afternoon.

A replica of Shakespeare's own theatre, the Globe, has been built in London, and stands in Southwark, almost exactly on the Bankside site of the original.

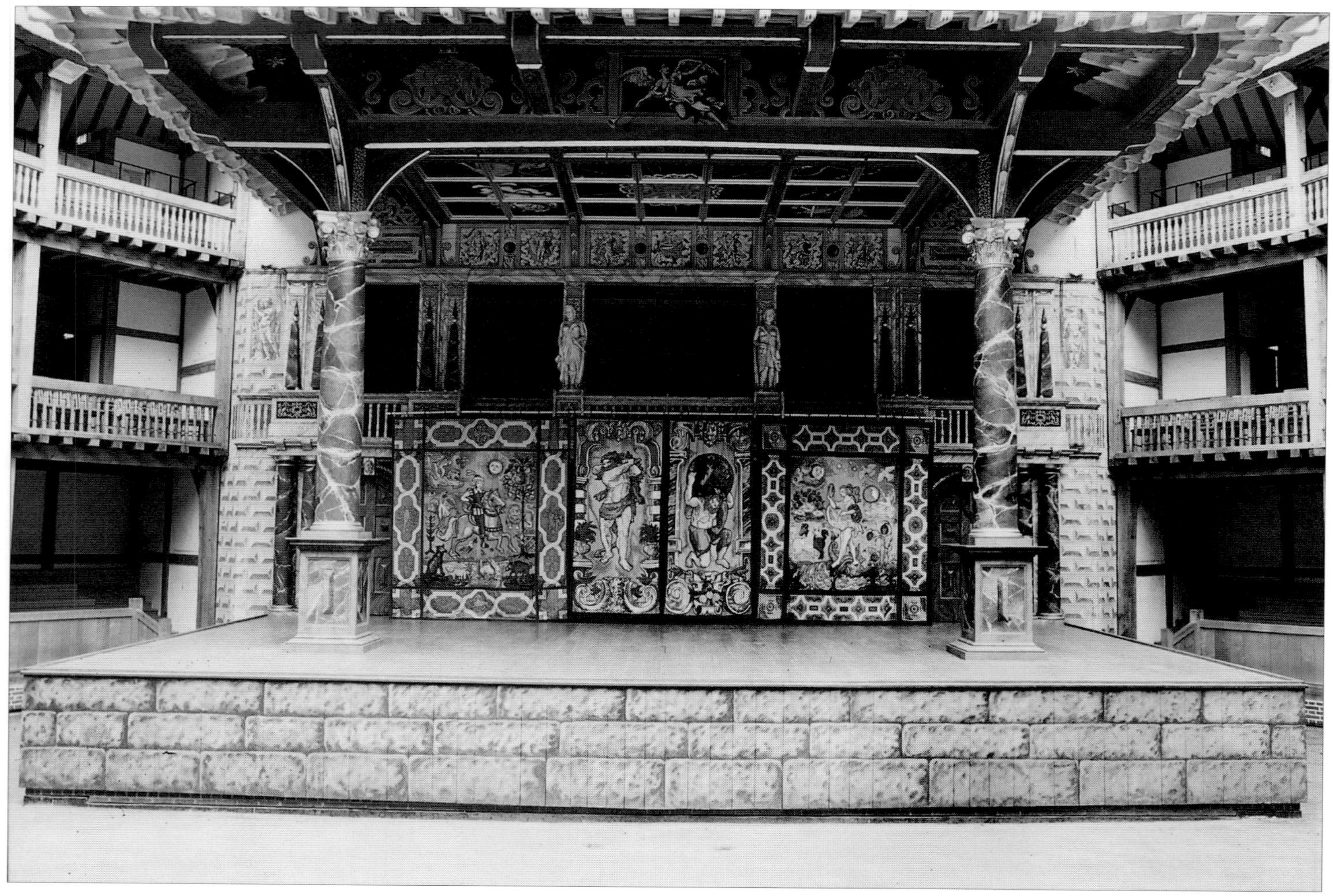

Shakespeare's Globe, Southwark, London, England. Photograph by Richard Kalina.

Further Reading

Editions: Excellent introductions to *Measure for Measure* are to be found in:

Bawcutt, Nigel, *Measure for Measure* (Oxford Shakespeare, 1991).
Gibbons, Brian, *Measure for Measure* (New Cambridge Shakespeare, 1991).

Critical Works:

Brown, J. Russell, *Shakespeare and His Comedies* (1957).
Cookson, L., and Loughrey, B., *Measure for Measure*, Longman Critical Essays (1991).
Foakes, R. A., *Shakespeare: The Dark Comedies to the Last Plays: From Satire to Celebration* (1971).
Hawkins, Harriett, *Measure for Measure* (1987).
Knight, G. Wilson, *The Wheel of Fire* (1930).
Leavis, F. R., *The Common Pursuit* (1953).
Rossiter, A. P., *Angel with Horns* (1961).
Stead, C. K., *Shakespeare's 'Measure for Measure': a Casebook* (Macmillan, 1971).

Sources:

Muir, Kenneth, *The Sources of Shakespeare's Plays* (London, 1977).

Additional background reading:

Bate, Jonathan, *The Genius of Shakespeare* (Picador [Macmillan], 1997).
Blake, N. F., *Shakespeare's Language: an Introduction* (London, 1983).
Gibson, Rex, *Shakespeare's Language* (Cambridge, 1997).
Honan, Park, *Shakespeare: A Life* (Oxford, 1998).
Muir, K., and Schoenbaum, S., *A New Companion to Shakespeare Studies* (Cambridge, 1971).
Langley, Andrew, *Shakespeare's Theatre* (Oxford, 1999).
Thomson, Peter, *Shakespeare's Theatre* (London, 1983).

William Shakespeare, 1564–1616

Elizabeth I was Queen of England when Shakespeare was born in 1564. He was the son of a tradesman who made and sold gloves in the small town of Stratford-upon-Avon, and he was educated at the grammar school in that town. Shakespeare did not go to university when he left school, but worked, perhaps, in his father's business. When he was eighteen he married Anne Hathaway, who became the mother of his daughter, Susanna, in 1583, and of twins in 1585.

There is nothing exciting, or even unusual, in this story; and from 1585 until 1592 there are no documents that can tell us anything at all about Shakespeare. But we have learned that in 1592 he was known in London, and that he had become both an actor and a playwright.

We do not know when Shakespeare wrote his first play, and indeed we are not sure of the order in which he wrote his works. If you look on page 139 at the list of his writings and their approximate dates, you will see how he started by writing plays on subjects taken from the history of England. No doubt this was partly because he was always an intensely patriotic man—but he was also a very shrewd business-man. He could see that the theatre audiences enjoyed being shown their own history, and it was certain that he would make a profit from this kind of drama.

The plays in the next group are mainly comedies, with romantic love-stories of young people who fall in love with one another, and at the end of the play marry and live happily ever after.

At the end of the sixteenth century the happiness disappears, and Shakespeare's plays become melancholy, bitter, and tragic. This change may have been caused by some sadness in the writer's life (one of his twins died in 1596). Shakespeare, however, was not the only writer whose works at this time were very serious. The whole of England was facing a crisis. Queen Elizabeth I was growing old. She was greatly loved, and the people were sad to think she must soon die; they were also afraid, for the queen had never married, and so there was no child to succeed her.

When James I came to the throne in 1603, Shakespeare continued to write serious drama—the great tragedies and the plays based on Roman history for which he is most famous. Finally, before he retired from the theatre, he wrote another set of comedies. These all have the same theme: they tell of happiness which is lost, and then found again.

Shakespeare returned from London to Stratford, his home town. He was rich and successful, and he owned one of the biggest houses in the town. He died in 1616.

Shakespeare also wrote two long poems, and a collection of sonnets. The sonnets describe two love-affairs, but we do not know who the lovers were. Although there are many public documents concerned with his career as a writer and a business-man, Shakespeare has hidden his personal life from us. A nineteenth-century poet, Matthew Arnold, addressed Shakespeare in a poem, and wrote 'We ask and ask—Thou smilest, and art still'.

There is not even a trustworthy portrait of the world's greatest dramatist.

Approximate order of composition of Shakespeare's works

Period	Comedies	History plays	Tragedies	Poems
I	Comedy of Errors	Henry VI, part 1	Titus Andronicus	
	Taming of the Shrew	Henry VI, part 2		
1594	Two Gentlemen of Verona	Henry VI, part 3		
		Richard III		Venus and Adonis
	Love's Labour's Lost	King John		Rape of Lucrece
II	Midsummer Night's Dream	Richard II	Romeo and Juliet	Sonnets
	Merchant of Venice	Henry IV, part 1		
1599	Merry Wives of Windsor	Henry IV, part 2		
	Much Ado About Nothing			
	As You Like It	Henry V		
III	Twelfth Night		Julius Caesar	
	Troilus and Cressida		Hamlet	
1608	Measure for Measure		Othello	
	All's Well That Ends Well		Timon of Athens	
			King Lear	
			Macbeth	
			Antony and Cleopatra	
			Coriolanus	
IV	Pericles			
	Cymbeline			
1613	The Winter's Tale			
	The Tempest	Henry VIII